*Current*
**CONTROVERSIES**

# Globalization

# Other books in the Current Controversies series

Alcoholism

Alternative Energy Sources

Cancer

Child Abuse

Conserving the Environment

The Elderly

Hate Crimes

Sexual Harassment

Suicide

Teenage Pregnancy and Parenting

Weapons of Mass Destruction

# Globalization

*Debra A. Miller, Book Editor*

**GREENHAVEN PRESS**

*An imprint of Thomson Gale, a part of The Thomson Corporation*

Detroit • New York • San Francisco • New Haven, Conn. • Waterville, Maine • London

# THOMSON

★ ™

# GALE

Christine Nasso, *Publisher*
Elizabeth Des Chenes, *Managing Editor*

© 2007 Thomson Gale, a part of The Thomson Corporation.

Thomson and Star logo are trademarks and Gale and Greenhaven Press are registered trademarks used herein under license.

*For more information, contact:*
Greenhaven Press
27500 Drake Rd.
Farmington Hills, MI 48331-3535
Or you can visit our Internet site at http://www.gale.com

Cover photograph reproduced by permission of Eddie Vincent.

LIBRARY OF CONGRESS CATALOGING-IN-PUBLICATION DATA

Globalization / Debra A. Miller, book editor.
    p. cm. -- (Current controversies)
    Includes bibliographical references and index.
    ISBN-13: 978-0-7377-3287-0 (hardcover)
    ISBN-10: 0-7377-3287-3 (hardcover)
    ISBN-13: 978-0-7377-3288-7 (pbk.)
    ISBN-10: 0-7377-3288-1 (pbk.)
    1. Globalization--Juvenile literature. I. Miller, Debra A.
    JZ1318.C845 2007
    303.48'2--dc22

                                      2006038691

Printed in the United States of America
10 9 8 7 6 5 4 3 2 1

# Contents

Foreword      **11**

Introduction      **14**

## Chapter 1: Will Globalization Hurt Workers?

Globalization: An Overview      **18**

*Mark Garnett*

The global integration of economies and cultures caused by recent technological changes is highly controversial, with supporters pointing to many benefits and critics warning of dire consequences.

### Yes: Globalization Will Hurt Workers

A Race to the Bottom for Workers and Workers' Rights      **24**

*Gus Tyler*

Globalization of the world economy creates incentives for companies to increase profits by decreasing labor costs, promoting a race to the bottom that depresses wages and creates unsafe workplaces for workers.

The Outsourcing of U.S. Jobs      **30**

*Trevor Gomberg*

Globalization is causing an increasing number of U.S. jobs to be outsourced to underdeveloped nations—a process that may eventually reduce the standard of living for many Americans.

### No: Globalization Will Not Hurt Workers

Globalization is an Opportunity for the U.S. Economy      **33**

*Robert T. Parry*

Overall, globalization creates as many jobs as it takes away, and displaced U.S. workers can be protected by providing unemployment insurance and training programs.

Job Losses from Globalization                                     **41**
Are Exaggerated
*Paul Swaim and Raymond Torres*
Globalization produces some job losses, but these are often exaggerated and can be dealt with by policy measures
that compensate job losers and increase their re-
employment chances.

## Chapter 2: Does Globalization Harm Developing Countries?

Chapter Preface                                                   **46**

### Yes: Globalization Harms Developing Countries

Unregulated Globalization Can Lead to                             **50**
Impoverishment for Developing Countries
*Lucky O. Imade*
In the absence of effective international rules and legal
systems to protect labor and the environment and prevent monopolies, globalization can lead to oppression,
exploitation, and impoverishment for many developing
countries.

Globalization Reforms Have Slowed                                 **58**
Economic Growth for Most Poor Countries
*Mark Weisbrot, Dean Baker, and David Rosnick*
Available economic data show that most developing
countries have experienced a sharply slower rate of economic growth during the last twenty years of globalization reforms.

The Concerns of Developing Countries Are                          **63**
Not Being Addressed by Global Trade Talks
*Michael Fleshman*
Global trade liberalization talks, launched at Doha, Qa-
tar, in 2001, have not produced the kinds of development
sought by developing nations to lift them out of poverty.

**No: Globalization Does Not Harm Developing Countries**

Multinational Corporations Do Not
Exploit Poor Countries                               **70**
*Jagdish Bhagwati*

Critics often claim that multinational corporations exploit poor countries by paying low wages and violating
labor rights but the evidence shows that globalization
does more good than harm.

Globalization Has Helped Many                        **75**
Developing Countries
*John L. Manzella*

Trade and globalization have improved the lives of billions of people in twenty-four developing countries that
have adopted free trade policies, by allowing their economies to catch up to those of rich countries.

Globalization's Pain for Poor Countries              **78**
Can Be Minimized
*Pranab Bardhan*

Whether globalization hurts or helps the poor in developing countries depends on the circumstances of each
country, but there are ways to maximize the benefits and
reduce the harm.

## Chapter 3: Will Globalization Destroy the Environment?

Globalization and the Environment:                   **89**
An Overview
*Radley Balko*

Free traders argue that short-term environmental damage may be necessary until countries can begin addressing environmental problems, but anti-globalists want immediate international standards to protect the world's
dwindling resources.

**Yes: Globalization Will Destroy the Environment**

The Pressures of Globalization Will Produce
Unprecedented Environmental Deterioration
    96

*James Gustave Speth*

Since the end of World War II, economic expansion has
produced enormous environmental damage, and globalized economic development can be expected to bring
about even more appalling economic consequences.

Environmental Damage Is Intrinsic to
the Globalization Process
    102

*Jerry Mander*

Globalization is a human creation that seeks to eliminate
impediments, such as environmental laws, that restrict
corporate access to resources and markets; environmental
damage therefore is an intrinsic part of the globalization
system.

In Mexico, Free Trade Has Led to Large-Scale
Environmental Degradation
    112

*Kevin P. Gallagher*

Proponents of the North American Free Trade Agreement (NAFTA) argued that free trade would improve the
environment in countries like Mexico, but ten years later,
environmental problems in Mexico have substantially
worsened.

Current Global Business Practices Harm
the Environment
    118

*Al Gore and David Blood*

Some global businesses are leading the way toward sustainable development of environmental resources, but
there is a long way to go and most companies still focus
on short-term investments and profits.

**No: Globalization Will Not Destroy
the Environment**

Free Trade Protects the Environment
    122

*Global Freedom to Trade Campaign*

Unrestricted trade will promote economic development
that will lift people in poor countries out of poverty,
thereby enabling them to improve health and improve
environmental protections.

NAFTA's Environmental Protections                131
Have Worked
    *Gustavo Vega-Canovas*
    NAFTA's environmental protections, embodied in the
    North American Agreement on Environmental Coopera-
    tion (NAAEC), have worked to allow citizens and envi-
    ronmental groups to challenge the negative environmen-
    tal effects of free trade policies.

Free Trade Will Not Hurt the Environment          139
if Trade Agreements Are Accompanied
by Environmental Standards
    *Nathan Johnson*
    The Free Trade Area of the Americas (FTAA) initiative
    raises legitimate concerns that American firms may try to
    take advantage of lax environmental standards in South
    American countries, but these can be addressed by in-
    cluding environmental standards in the agreement.

## Chapter 4: Is Globalization a Threat to Democracy?

Chapter Preface                                   146

**Yes: Globalization Is a Threat to Democracy**

Global Capitalism Is Subverting Democracy         150
    *Noreen Hertz*
    Corporations are becoming global giants that wield more
    political power than elected politicians, a silent takeover
    that is eroding democracy around the world.

Globalization Presents a Serious Challenge        156
to Democratic Sovereignty and the
Democratic Nation-State
    *John Fonte*
    Globalization has spawned international agencies and
    non-governmental organizations (NGOs) that are push-
    ing for changes that could override the national sover-
    eignty of democratic states.

The Spread of Global Free-Market                    **165**
Democracy Causes Ethnic Violence
  *Amy Chua*
  Because free markets and democracy often benefit one
  minority group instead of the majority of the population, globalization can exacerbate economic inequities
  and result in political instability and violence.

**No: Globalization Is Not a Threat to Democracy**

Globalization Promotes Democracy Both               **171**
Directly and Indirectly
  *Jagdish Bhagwati*
  Global economic reforms promote democracy because
  people who experience economic freedoms then seek
  greater control over other decisions that affect their lives.

Global Economic Development Is a Tool for           **176**
Encouraging Democracy
  *Daniel T. Griswold*
  Increased global trade and economic development in
  less-developed countries promote democratic freedoms
  by opening societies to new technologies, communications, and democratic ideas.

The Nation-State Will Survive Globalization         **182**
  *Martin Wolf*
  Countries that choose to participate in the global economic system must accept some constraints on sovereign
  powers, but nation-states will always be necessary to provide stability, security, and benefits to citizens.

Glossary                                            **190**

Chronology                                          **193**

Organizations to Contact                            **198**

Bibliography                                        **208**

Index                                               **213**

# Foreword

By definition, controversies are "discussions of questions in which opposing opinions clash" (Webster's Twentieth Century Dictionary, Unabridged). Few would deny that controversies are a pervasive part of the human condition and exist on virtually every level of human enterprise. Controversies transpire between individuals and among groups, within nations and between nations. Controversies supply the grist necessary for progress by providing challenges and challengers to the status quo. They also create atmospheres where strife and warfare can flourish. A world without controversies would be a peaceful world; but it also would be, by and large, static and prosaic.

## The Series' Purpose

The purpose of the Current Controversies series is to explore many of the social, political, and economic controversies dominating the national and international scenes today. Titles selected for inclusion in the series are highly focused and specific. For example, from the larger category of criminal justice, Current Controversies deals with specific topics such as police brutality, gun control, white collar crime, and others. The debates in Current Controversies also are presented in a useful, timeless fashion. Articles and book excerpts included in each title are selected if they contribute valuable, long-range ideas to the overall debate. And wherever possible, current information is enhanced with historical documents and other relevant materials. Thus, while individual titles are current in focus, every effort is made to ensure that they will not become quickly outdated. Books in the Current Controversies series will remain important resources for librarians, teachers, and students for many years.

In addition to keeping the titles focused and specific, great care is taken in the editorial format of each book in the series. Book introductions and chapter prefaces are offered to provide background material for readers. Chapters are organized around several key questions that are answered with diverse opinions representing all points on the political spectrum. Materials in each chapter include opinions in which authors clearly disagree as well as alternative opinions in which authors may agree on a broader issue but disagree on the possible solutions. In this way, the content of each volume in Current Controversies mirrors the mosaic of opinions encountered in society. Readers will quickly realize that there are many viable answers to these complex issues. By questioning each author's conclusions, students and casual readers can begin to develop the critical thinking skills so important to evaluating opinionated material.

Current Controversies is also ideal for controlled research. Each anthology in the series is composed of primary sources taken from a wide gamut of informational categories, including periodicals, newspapers, books, United States and foreign government documents, and the publications of private and public organizations. Readers will find factual support for reports, debates, and research papers covering all areas of important issues. In addition, an annotated table of contents, an index, a book and periodical bibliography, and a list of organizations to contact are included in each book to expedite further research.

Perhaps more than ever before in history, people are confronted with diverse and contradictory information. During the Persian Gulf War, for example, the public was not only treated to minute-to-minute coverage of the war, it was also inundated with critiques of the coverage and countless analyses of the factors motivating U.S. involvement. Being able to sort through the plethora of opinions accompanying today's major issues, and to draw one's own conclusions, can be a complicated and frustrating struggle. It is the editors' hope that Current Controversies will help readers with this struggle.

# Introduction

*"One of the deepest fears . . . is that globalization may be promoting an essentially American and materialistic culture that threatens local, traditional cultures around the world."*

In the early morning darkness on Tuesday, November 30, 1999, activists from around the world converged on the downtown streets of Seattle, Washington, determined to send a message to the world that the current system of globalization must be changed. The protest was organized to disrupt a meeting of the World Trade Organization (WTO), an international organization set up to promote and regulate global trade—an entity that has been described as "the most powerful unelected organization on the planet." The generally peaceful crowd rapidly grew to close to 50,000 people and police quickly moved in with teargas, rubber bullets, and pepper spray. Chaos ensued and the WTO meeting was cancelled.

The 1999 Seattle demonstration and subsequent protests in various parts of the world have caused many people to re-examine the human effects of globalization. Indeed, globalization—sometimes broadly viewed as the growing interconnectedness of people around the world but more often narrowly defined as global trade—has become one of the most hotly debated topics in the twenty-first century. Experts agree that globalization brings many benefits, most notably lower prices on consumer goods and dramatically increased access to information. At the same time, however, critics charge that globalization has been a process dominated by a handful of U.S. and Western multinational corporations that, unrestrained by legal, moral, or social concerns and motivated only by greed, seek profits for shareholders at the expense of local and national concerns.

One of the deepest fears of critics, for example, is that globalization may be promoting an essentially American and materialistic culture that threatens local, traditional cultures around the globe. Some call it the "Wal-Mart," "McDonalds," or "Coca-Cola" effect, in which large U.S. corporations move into nations, many of them with rich and often ancient histories, to promote U.S. products to local consumers. These cultural imports are often very popular; indeed, as international affairs professor David Rothkop noted in a 1997 *Foreign Policy* article, "American music, American movies, American television, and American software are so dominant, so sought after, and so visible that they are now available literally everywhere on the Earth." Because American influences tend to draw people away from traditional arts and lifestyles, however, critics charge that they often dilute, corrupt, or destroy local culture and diversity.

By portraying a westernized way of life that many people in other parts of the world view as secular and materialistic, American cultural imports also can threaten local religious or social values, causing conflict within societies as well as friction with the West. The prominence of U.S. companies in global trade, some experts claim, is already leading to a backlash of anti-American sentiment around the world—a phenomenon that some critics argue may be behind recent incidents of Islamic terrorism and violence against innocent Americans. As *New York Times* columnist Thomas Friedman wrote in his 2000 book on globalization, *The Lexus and the Olive Tree*, "The greatest danger to the United States today is Superempowered individuals who hate America more than ever because of globalization."

Globalization's advocates, on the other hand, argue that global trade creates wealth that allows people to better save and celebrate indigenous art, music, crafts, and literature that otherwise might be lost. Global trade can also enrich local cultures by providing new ideas that can be absorbed into and mixed with traditional influences. Economist Tyler Cowen elaborated on this idea at a 2003 book forum organized by the Cato Institute: "Trade has made different countries, different regions, more creative, given us more diversity. . . . The blossoming of world literature . . . the bookstore, the printing press, the advent of cinema around the globe are all cases in which trade has made different countries . . . more creative." Some supporters even point to the emergence of a new global culture, in which people are free to choose elements from many different cultures. Almost everywhere on earth, people now are exposed not only to a wide variety of consumer products, but also to many different types of foods, clothing, music, visual arts, religions, and cultural traditions that they can incorporate as they choose into their lives.

Pro-globalists argue too that global trade, instead of disrupting social and religious networks, is actually causing many people to more deeply embrace traditions and religions as a source of identity and meaning in the midst of today's changing world. Furthermore, the decline of some cultural distinctions, such as racist, ethnic, or sexist values in some religions or cultures, may be a necessary, positive development that will lead to a more tolerant, multicultural global society.

The effect of globalization on culture, however, is just one of the many debates presented by the authors in *Current Controversies: Globalization*. The authors give their perspectives on several other important aspects of this phenomenon, including globalization's effect on the economy, the environment, and on democracy itself. Whether globalization unites or threatens cultures, societies, nations, and the environment is the question that lies at the heart of the globalization controversy.

# CHAPTER 1

# Will Globalization Hurt Workers?

# Globalization: An Overview

*Mark Garnett*

**About the author**: *Mark Garnett is an Honorary Fellow in the Department of Politics at the University of Leicester in Great Britain.*

In the last two decades 'globalisation' has emerged as a familiar term in political discussions—in the media as well as in academic contexts. It is often claimed that globalisation is a process which affects all our lives to an increasing extent. We are living in a globalised economy which has a profound impact on our activities as consumers and as workers. Our cultural assumptions, too, are supposedly being globalised: in music, food, fashion and film, people across the world are coming under the same influences and sharing similar experiences.

Globalisation is a highly controversial term. Those who believe that something radical and new is happening define the process in different ways. Some argue that it is a beneficial phenomenon, while critics claim that it encourages exploitation and even threatens the future of our planet. Others suggest that it is nothing new, or that its effects have been exaggerated. It is impossible to reach any firm conclusions on such a huge topic, so the task here is to try to understand the issues and to provide a critical analysis of the leading perspectives.

## The Causes of Globalisation

Both critics and supporters of globalisation agree that the process has been driven by technological changes in communication and transport. The first industrial revolution ensured that messages could be sent over great distances at the speed of a railway engine or steam ship; but in the contemporary

Mark Garnett, "Globalisation," *Politics Review*, vol. 14, February 2005, pp. 26–27. Copyright 2005 Philip Allan Updates. Reproduced by permission.

world these means of communication seem intolerably slow. Thanks to satellites and the internet, ideas and information can be disseminated throughout the world at the flick of a switch or the press of a button.

While these developments have an obvious effect across a wide range of activities, the potential for change is arguably greatest in the economic sphere. In the past, industrial production had to be located close to sources of raw materials or the most lucrative markets. These factors are still important, but many large firms now have the option of moving to areas where labour costs are relatively low. Increased automation in the production process, particularly associated with the use of computer technology, means that identical products can be made almost anywhere on earth before being shipped to the areas of highest demand. Even parts of the service sector now have a global reach: British customers telephoning for advice from their banks or for information on local rail timetables can find themselves speaking to someone thousands of miles away.

*All governments now have to gear their economic policies to global developments which they cannot hope to control.*

## The Effects of Globalisation

The most obvious effect of this process has been to undermine the traditional role of the nation state. All governments now have to gear their economic policies to global developments which they cannot hope to control. Increasingly, they make decisions which are intended to boost the competitive position of their countries in relation to global competitors. In Britain, for example, recent governments have recognised that they cannot compete with relatively low cost economies like China, and argue that future prosperity will depend on a highly skilled, well motivated workforce.

Another effect of the changes associated with globalisation is a tendency to see the countries of the world as increasingly interdependent. News travels faster and further, so that a major event in one country will be reported extensively throughout the globe. Furthermore, developments abroad will tend to have a much greater relevance to the situation at home. The most obvious example of this is the impact of terrorist atrocities in places like New York, Bali and Madrid, persuading people to think again about their attitude to air travel and forcing governments across the world to reappraise their security policies. Interdependency means that economic problems in one country can have a serious effect elsewhere.

---

*Interdependency means that economic problems in one country can have a serious effect elsewhere.*

---

## The Benefits of Globalisation

Supporters of globalisation claim that interdependency brings many benefits.

- In the economic sphere, global competition means that consumers enjoy the widest possible choice, at the lowest prices. Relatively speaking, everyone benefits; even low paid workers in the 'developing world' enjoy far better living standards.

- As citizens in the global marketplace become more prosperous and learn about conditions in other countries, they demand the political and civil rights associated with liberalism, such as the right to vote and to express opinions without fear of prosecution. Even a country like China, which is still officially communist, encourages free enterprise and will find it increasingly difficult to resist demands for political reform.

- As national boundaries dissolve, so do long held prejudices based on creeds and colours. Individual human beings are now able to judge one another on their own merits, regardless of their origins.

- The English language is either the first or second language for most 'global citizens'. This is an accident of history, a legacy of the British empire and the more recent rise of the USA. The USA is a 'global community'—a country which welcomes immigrants who are prepared to accept liberal values. The dominance of the English language is an invaluable aid to communication, which reflects the power of freedom rather than the interests of any one country.

- The twentieth century was dominated by wars between nation-states. We can look forward to a future without wars—what one US commentator, Francis Fukuyama, has hailed as 'the end of history'.

## The Perils of Globalisation

Critics of globalisation paint a deeply contrasting picture.

- 'Global competition' is no such thing. The rich countries of the developed world are able to exploit the rest. For example, they dictate the terms of trade in agriculture, protecting their domestic producers by imposing tariffs on imports from other countries.

- Far from increasing the rights of people across the world, globalisation denies ordinary citizens a meaningful voice. Power has passed into the hands of unaccountable multinational corporations like General Motors, Coca-Cola and McDonald's, and even where political parties are allowed to compete they tend to offer identical policies. Among other things, the need to compete with low paid workers abroad has allowed governments to reduce the rights of Western trade unionists.

- Although Western governments approve of the 'free' movement of goods (on their own definition of freedom), they look less favourably on the idea of free movement of people. Greater communication between nations has exposed citizens of developing countries to the enormous prosperity of the West, but if they want to migrate with their families they will meet obstructions which are being increased rather than reduced. Most Western countries still discriminate heavily against black and Asian immigrants, and since 11 September 2001 Muslims have come under increasing suspicion.

- The dominance of the English language reflects the awesome power of the USA, which in practice has caused even more suffering in the developing world than the exploitative British empire.

- The incidence of violent conflict, far from diminishing, is increasing as the USA struggles to impose its own idea of 'order' on distant nations. One trade which has been 'global' in scale for many years is the provision of modern weaponry by the developed world to sympathetic states or rebel movements. These weapons have fuelled conflict, either within or between nations. In the future, nations will engage in increasingly desperate conflicts over vital raw materials, particularly the oil which underpins the Western way of life.

- Finally, the opponents of globalisation argue that the spread of Western ideas throughout the world threatens to bring human life to an end. Although some scientists reject predictions of environmental catastrophe, it is difficult to find any reputable commentator who thinks that increased economic activity will benefit the world. The anti-globalisation movement argues that this is one respect in which countries really are interdependent, because pollution knows no boundaries. They are not surprised by the failure of Western countries to take action, because they think that 'globalisation' is simply a grandiose term for US self-interest.

## A Complex Phenomenon

Even from this brief survey we can appreciate the importance and complexity of 'globalisation'. It can arouse extreme emotions—on both sides of the argument—especially since '9/11' and the US led war on Iraq, both of which can only be understood in the context of globalisation. This makes it difficult to be 'objective', but that should not prevent us from reaching an understanding of the issues and arguments.

One point which can be made is that globalisation is not as new as some of its supporters claim. After all, between 1914 and 1918 and 1939 and 1945 there were major conflicts which were not misnamed 'world wars'. Before these wars, the colonial powers of Europe fought against each other in distant lands, and the victors usually tried to impose their ideas on the native populations. Even before the whole of the globe had been 'discovered' by Western explorers, national governments were keen to push their trading activities as far as possible. It seems reasonable to argue that the word 'globalisation' has caught on in recent years because technological developments have massively increased the scale of a phenomenon which was well known to previous generations.

# A Race to the Bottom for Workers and Workers' Rights

*Gus Tyler*

**About the author**: *Gus Tyler is a prominent labor leader, a former assistant president of the International Ladies' Garment Workers' Union (ILGWU), and a prolific writer and syndicated columnist.*

For a couple of decades there has been a slow but steady deterioration of the spine of the U.S. economy: manufacturing. The downward trend started in labor-intensive industries like apparel, shoes, rubber wear, dolls, toys, and novelties. It spread first to electronic assembly, and then to capital-intensive businesses: autos, steel, pharmaceuticals, computers. In 1979 there were 21 million jobs in American manufacturing, constituting 30 percent of all U.S. employment. If that percentage had persisted, there would be 39 million such jobs today. Instead, the 2001 total was 17 million.

The dramatic shortfall is not reflected in unemployment statistics because of the service sector's growth. But those jobs—replenishing shelves in a supermarket, cutting grass, cleaning a home or hospital—usually pay the minimum wage. A typical autoworker earns, with fringe benefits, about $50,000 a year. At the minimum wage, a person working 40 hours a week for 50 weeks earns $10,300 before taxes. With roughly 70 per cent of the economy depending upon purchases by workers, a decline in the effective demand of blue-collar families means a decline in the customer base our market economy depends on.

Gus Tyler, "Combating the Perils of Globalization," *The New Leader*, vol. 86, January–February 2003, pp. 15–17. Copyright © 2003 by The American Labor Conference on International Affairs, Inc. All rights reserved. Reproduced by permission.

## A Drive for Cheap Labor

A common explanation for the shrinkage of manufacturing jobs is that technological advancements have made it possible to meet demand with fewer employees. This would be a valid analysis if the multinational corporations had reduced the number of people on their payrolls. Most however, have actually done the opposite—but moved their operations to countries where cheap child and even slave labor is readily available.

The hope was that these new workers would awaken and organize to secure higher wages, so that eventually they would not only improve their own circumstances but become buyers of products made in the United States. Sadly, quite the opposite has been happenning. A 2000 Central Intelligence Agency report projecting global trends for 15 years arrived at the following conclusions:

> The rising tide of the global economy will create many winners, but will not lift all boats. It will spawn conflicts at home and abroad, ensuring an even wider gap between regional winners and losers than exists today. Globalization's evolution will be rocky, marked by chronic financial volatility and a widening economic divide. Regions, countries, and groups feeling left behind will face deepening economic stagnation, political instability and cultural alienation. They will foster political, ethnic, ideological, and religious extremism, along with the violence that often accompanies it.

The CIA was not alone. During the previous year the World Bank declared: "Globalization appears to increase poverty and inequality. The costs of adjusting to greater openness are borne exclusively by the poor, regardless of how long the adjustment takes."

Last March [2002] the United Nations International Conference on Financing for Development, held in Monterrey, Mexico, confirmed the gloomy global picture. Representatives of the world's great industrial powers and economic agencies agreed that conditions in the underdeveloped countries are worse now than they were just after World War II, when the drive for "development" started.

## The Green Revolution

Four factors account for where we stand and where we are headed economically. The first is the mechanization of agriculture. In the postwar expansion, U.S. and European agribusiness brought the applauded "green revolution" to foreign lands. Technological improvements deprived millions of farmers and peasants of their income and their homes. The impact was not limited to the so-called Third World. In the 20 years following World War II, the automation of farming in the American South annually drove out about 1 million agricultural workers and owners of small farms. Luckily, the U.S. economy was then expanding and many found industrial jobs in Northern cities.

In the poorer countries, too, farmhands moved to urban areas in search of employment. But they were soon literally starving. Western manufacturing corporations licked their chops and cheered. Here were millions of people (actually a few billion) ready to do for pennies what had been costing relatively heavy dollars. Management forces seized the opportunity.

## Technology and Communications Advancements

That was made possible by the second factor: the mobility and reach of business. When Englishman David Ricardo wrote his masterpiece, *Principles of Political Economy and Taxation* (1817), he posed a rhetorical question: What would happen if a British textile merchant took his know-how to Portugal and paid local wages? Such competition, said Ricardo, would ruin the British textile industry. But, he added, the entrepreneur would never be able to pull it off, because he could not personally oversee what was happening in Portugal; he would not know the language and customs, let alone the law.

---

*The "race to the bottom" for ever cheaper and more docile labor can be graphically charted.*

---

The situation changed radically after World War II, of course, with the technological transformation of communications, transportation, materials handling, and data processing. Before long the headquarters of a company could keep watch over every move made by its far-flung factories, could communicate instantaneously with them, and could ship products halfway around the world in a matter of hours. As a result, some multinational corporations now have over 100 plants scattered throughout the globe.

## The Race to the Bottom

The "race to the bottom" for ever cheaper and more docile labor can be graphically charted: Early in the postwar era American, European and Japanese businesses began to open plants, or hire contractors, in Taiwan. As the island's labor market tightened, workers began to make demands and costs rose. The multinationals then started to move their operations to coastal mainland China. When wages pushed upward there, a shift was made to China's interior, where inexpensive workers were plentiful. At the moment indications are that the price of labor is rising again, so the ever alert corporations are turning their attention to Africa.

## The Failure of Global Institutions

A third factor that has contributed to the worsening state of global economic affairs is the uneven performance of agencies created at Bretton Woods in 1944—the International Monetary Fund (IMF) and the International Bank for Reconstruction and Development (now called the World Bank). Originally, the IMF was charged with stabilizing exchange rates to prevent a country from weakening its currency to make imports more expensive and exports cheaper. But that hasn't stopped it from assuming a larger role in running—and ruining—the economies of needy nations.

---

*Although the [globalization] prescription is painful for working people to swallow, the international corporations love it.*

---

Typically, the government of country X has been borrowing heavily because it is on the verge of bankruptcy. In desperation, it turns to the IMF for a loan. The IMF says it will only assent under certain conditions, the foremost being unmitigated "austerity." X must sharply reduce the cost of its products, whether agricultural or industrial, which means keeping wages low and resisting union demands. It must also minimize spending on social programs: food relief, housing, health care, unemployment benefits, Social Security, etc. In addition, it has to keep the currency weak, to insure that its products will attract consumers abroad. X will thereby acquire enough foreign capital to start paying back other countries and the IMF.

Although the prescription is painful for working people to swallow, the international corporations love it. After all, it gives them a big pool of hungry citizens willing to sweat their lives away for close to nothing, and being ordered by the state not to make trouble.

## U.S. and European Agricultural Subsidies

The fourth factor, in some respects an extension of the first, is the excessive support provided by the United States and Europe for domestic agricultural production. These subsidies are so large that the crops they encourage can be sold on the world market below cost and still yield a profit. Consequently, farm exports to Third World countries make it impossible for their farmers to compete.

The danger is that things will one day come full circle: The collapse of manufacturing in the industrial nations has led to slowdowns that have led to recessions that could be the prelude to depressions. At present the U.S. is least affected, much of Europe is experiencing double-digit unemployment, and Japan is in deep trouble.

## Prospects for Improvement

Neither the distress in the developing countries nor the stress building up in the developed ones has gone unnoticed. The dramatic "Battle in Seattle," pitting activists against the World Trade Organization (WTO) at its April 1999 meeting, and subsequent protests in Prague, Washington, D.C., and Genoa, have attracted widespread attention to the issue. The demonstrators vented their fear of the effects of globalization as it is now manipulated by pressure from the multinational corporations and the presumably protective international financial entities. But so far the somewhat amorphous "antiglobalization" movement has not put forward a coherent program for improving matters.

That task is difficult, primarily because there is no global government that can function the way national governments did, say, after the Great Depression. By establishing a balance between the public and private sectors—and thereby balancing the capacity to produce and the capacity to consume—the large industrial democracies were able to forestall old-fashioned depressions for over a half-century. They were successful because they had the authority to tell business what it was and was not allowed to do. Today, by contrast, big companies thumb their noses at their governments as they carry on operations outside the geographic limits of their native lands.

# The Outsourcing of U.S. Jobs

*Trevor Gomberg*

**About the author***: Trevor Gomberg is a student at Binghamton University's School of Management and a winner of a scholarship from the Southern Tier New York Chapter of the National Contract Management Association (NCMA) for his essay on the outsourcing topic.*

We have all heard of the benefits of the global economy. Economics teaches us about the benefits of comparative advantage—each country makes whatever product for which it is best suited. Today, this globalization trend continues, as we see more and more U.S. jobs being shipped offshore.

Specific activities include actions such as downsizing, which is becoming more than just a market fluctuation and rather a road toward an uncertain future for corporate jobs. Information technology jobs in particular are being sent over to nations like India, where labor that might cost $100 here would get done for one-fifth of the cost. A recent *Business Week* article portrayed a 26-year-old computer engineer eager to start his $10,000/year job developing computer chips—a completely insufficient salary for the job by U.S. standards of living.

## The Staggering Proportions of Outsourcing

In an era when companies are trying their hardest to secure strong profits, this course of action might seem tempting. But, there comes a point, however, when an ethical decision must be made, regarding whether U.S. companies should be sacrificing so many loyal workers at home just to increase their bottom line. Just look at a local example—IBM played an integral part in the Sourthern Tier New York and employed many residents when it had a strong presence years ago in Endicott. Today, its size here has shrunk substantially. For the United States at large, the Bureau of Labor Statistics reported a 5.6-percent unemployment rate . . . [in] January 2004— which translates to more than 8 million people. These statistics make the prospects for those seeking employment rather daunting.

From the analysis perspective of comparative advantage, different countries produce the goods and provide the services for which they are best suited. Resources and labor dictate what country is best suited for certain forms of production. The problem we are facing today is that we are losing hold on what used to be our greatest strengths in the world market— manufacturing and industry. In the meantime, other countries have bolstered their efforts, and so now we have production outsourcing (e.g., car manufacturing in Mexico) as becoming the norm. As service and skilled labor jobs go offshore, line manager positions also must be placed elsewhere.

---

*Jobs in this country have become more competitive, as U.S. jobs are increasingly trickling away to underdeveloped nations, where costs are lower and returns higher.*

---

Strong prospects for growth in India and China are driving many U.S. jobs eastward. China's boom in tech-driven cities such as Shanghai and Chonquing are making the destinations attractive, aside from their phenomenal economic growth rates. India is utilizing its strength through its knowledge of English, which is almost spoken as widely as Hindi.

White-collar jobs on Wall Street are also being exported, where quantitative analysis work can be done just as efficiently, and for much less. Technical support has been routed abroad now for many years—especially to India, where time is 10.5 hours ahead of Eastern Standard Time. With companies boasting 24/7 service hotlines, time zone differences prove to be one viable solution for handling customer needs.

The statistics are truly staggering. Roughly 61,000 jobs are moving offshore today from business operations. That number is likely to grow to 348,000 in a decade. In management, where 37,000 jobs are moving off today, almost 300,000 will relocate to developing economies within the same period. Even accounting is being affected—overseas jobs that are done for tax work and the preparation of company financial statements. It is speculated that auditing will be the only segment of the profession that might be left unscathed.

## The Future?

Jobs in this country have become more competitive, as U.S. jobs are increasingly trickling away to underdeveloped nations, where costs are lower and returns higher. College graduates are already having a hard time finding jobs—many are being forced to consider gaining more credentials and certifications to get a competitive edge, while they sideline the inactive job market.

The future is questionable for business students and those of other fields, too. As the stock market continues to improve and unemployment drops, even negligibly, we have to wonder if jobs will be created to satisfy a demand for work posed by experienced professionals and college graduates. However, cutting corners cannot be the only way to cure fiscal woes; top-line growth must remain strong to ensure long-term survival.

It will be up to companies to reverse this underestimated trend in job outsourcing. Government intervention may also be the key, punishing the companies that lose jobs and granting incentives to those that keep jobs available for U.S. workers. Or, perhaps aggregate salaries and the standard of living at home will have to plummet to keep our jobs from going abroad.

Frankly, globalization has never been such a scary thought.

# Globalization is an Opportunity for the U.S. Economy

*Robert T. Parry*

**About the author**: *Robert T. Parry is the president and chief executive officer of the Federal Reserve Bank of San Francisco, one of twelve locations of the nation's central bank, which manages the nation's money system and regulates the country's banks.*

In the discussions about jobs, a lot of attention has focused on trade and terms such as "globalization," "outsourcing," and "offshoring." The concern, of course, is that a free-trade environment is letting good jobs drain from the U.S. economy and wind up in China, India, and other countries where workers command much lower salaries. In the extreme, some would like to see restraints on trade to protect those jobs and halt the globalization trend. Whether globalization is a threat or an opportunity for the U.S. economy is a big question with serious ramifications. . . .

## Why Are Most Economists in Favor of Free Trade?

Basically, the argument is that *everyone* benefits when countries specialize in the type of production at which they're relatively most efficient. Consider this analogy with the family: No family tries to make everything that it eats, wears, and enjoys. If it's cheaper to buy something or have someone else do something, that's what a family does. Then individual family members can concentrate on becoming good at their jobs in order to pay for what they buy.

Robert T. Parry, "Globalization: Threat or Opportunity for the U.S. Economy?" Federal Reserve Bank of San Francisco Economic Letter 2004-12, May 21, 2004. The opinions expressed in this article do not necessarily reflect the views of the management of the Federal Reserve Bank of San Francisco, or of the Governors of the Federal Reserve System. Reproduced by permission.

A nation is no different. If it costs less to make certain products abroad than it does in the U.S., then it's difficult to argue that U.S. consumers and U.S. companies should pay more for those products from U.S. producers. Instead, it makes sense to purchase those products more cheaply from abroad, whether they're hard goods, like VCRs, or services, like call centers. Then we can devote our resources to producing and exporting those goods where we have a relative advantage. The result is a twofold benefit—greater efficiency and lower costs for U.S. firms and consumers.

---

*Outsourcing is simply contracting out functions that had been done in-house, a longtime U.S. practice.*

---

## What Are "Outsourcing" and "Offshoring"?

In its broadest sense, outsourcing is simply contracting out functions that had been done in-house, a longtime U.S. practice. When a car manufacturer in Michigan buys brake pads from an intermediate supplier in Ohio rather than produce them in-house, that's outsourcing. When a company replaces its cleaning and cafeteria workers with an outside contractor who does the same services more cheaply, *that's* outsourcing. When a company contracts out its payroll, accounting, and software operations, that's outsourcing. Clearly, outsourcing can result in job losses if the outside supplier is more efficient and uses fewer workers.

---

*Each year, some 15 million jobs are lost for all kinds of reasons.*

---

Offshoring has been referred to as the global cousin of outsourcing. Instead of turning to domestic providers, firms may decide to purchase a good or service from overseas providers because of lower costs. Offshoring, too, has a long history in U.S. manufacturing; for example, firms in Mexico supply seat covers and wiper blades to Detroit automakers. What appears to be new about offshoring is that it's affecting workers in the service sector who never expected to see foreign competition for their jobs—data managers, computer programmers, medical transcriptionists, and the like.

How much offshoring is going on? That's difficult to say. We don't have official statistics, and there are a lot of unsettled measurement issues. But a couple of estimates that have gotten some press recently both suggest that the U.S. lost 100,000–170,000 jobs to foreign workers between 2000 and 2003. Those numbers sound high until you put them in the context of all the job turnover that occurs every year in the U.S. Each year, some 15 million jobs are lost for all kinds of reasons—voluntary employment changes, layoffs, firings, and so on. And in a growing economy, every year even more jobs are created.

---

*Even as the U.S. "loses" jobs when our companies send operations offshore, we also "gain" jobs as foreign corporations invest here.*

---

## Globalization Also Produces Jobs in the United States

The answer to this question will focus on three important issues that are sometimes neglected in the discussion. First, globalization means that economic activity flows in both directions; although we may lose jobs to foreign workers, we also may gain jobs and boost economic activity. For example, data suggest that, in terms of office work, the U.S. *insources* far more than it *outsources*; that is, just as U.S. firms use the services of foreigners, foreign firms make even greater use of the services of U.S. residents. "Office work" refers to the category of business, professional, and technical services that includes computer programming, telecommunications, legal services, banking, engineering, management consulting, call centers, data entry, and other private services. In 2003, we bought about $77 billion worth of those services from foreigners, but the value of the services we *sold* to foreigners was far higher, over $130 billion.

Here's another set of interesting numbers. Between 1991 and 2001, U.S.-based multinationals created close to 3 million jobs overseas. But they also created 5-1/2 million jobs inside the U.S.—an increase of about 30% in payrolls. That's a significantly faster rate of job growth than purely domestic companies generated. And it shows that you can't assume that a job created overseas necessarily means one isn't created here. For example, expanding an overseas network frequently means you have to hire more workers in the U.S., too—people in management, logistics, research and development, and international IT [information technology].

Here's a final set of numbers. According to the Commerce Department, even as the U.S. "loses" jobs when our companies send operations offshore, we also "gain" jobs as foreign corporations invest here. Specifically, foreign firms employed almost 6-1/2 million workers in the U.S. In 2001—up from about 5 million in 1991; these workers included highly paid Honda and Mercedes-Benz workers in the auto industry. There are plenty of other examples. In 2006, Toyota will employ 2,000 people building cars in San Antonio. Samsung is investing $500 million to expand its semiconductor plant in Austin, Texas. And Novartis is moving its R&D operation from Switzerland to Massachusetts.

## Global Trade Enlarges Markets for U.S. Goods

My second point is that open trade creates opportunities in the U.S by helping foreign economies become stronger. As incomes grow in other countries, so does their demand for goods and services, many of which those countries will not be able to produce—just as the U.S. does not. This rise in foreign demand for imports is an opportunity for U.S. firms to compete to provide those products. And it would be a shame to miss that opportunity because of trade barriers our policymakers erected. It would mean lost export sales and lost jobs in those sectors.

Finally, globalization can help increase productivity growth in the U.S. The example of offshoring's effect on the spread of IT in the U.S. and, therefore, on our economic growth illustrates the point. According to one estimate, the globalized production of IT hardware—that is, the offshoring of computer-related manufacturing, such as Dell computer factories in China—reduced the prices of computer and telecommunications equipment by 10%–30%. These price declines boosted the spread of IT throughout the U.S. economy and raised both productivity and growth.

Offshoring offers the potential to lower the prices of IT software and services as well. This will promote the further spread of IT—and of new business processes that take advantage of cheap IT. It also will create jobs for U.S. workers to design and implement IT packages for a range of industries and companies. Although some jobs are at risk, the same trends that make offshoring possible are creating new opportunities—and new jobs—throughout the U.S. economy. . . .

## The Importance of Productivity and a Flexible Workforce

Over the past two years, U.S. productivity in the nonfarm business sector has grown at a 4.8% annual rate. In the short term, this increased productivity has let businesses satisfy the demand for their output without having to hire new workers on net. So, it appears that this extraordinary surge of increased efficiency in our economy explains much more about the jobs situation than offshoring, outsourcing, or globalization does.

Although, clearly, productivity creates pain for workers who are displaced, most economists agree that higher productivity is a good thing for the economy. Why? Because, in the long run, higher productivity is the only way to create higher standards of living across the economy. The American worker's ability to produce more goods and services per hour has been the key to the U.S. economy's surprising success throughout its history. Consider the manufacturing and agricultural sectors, where more output can now be produced with fewer workers. The same trend has occurred in services: the U.S. used to have lots of elevator operators, telephone operators, bank tellers, and gas station attendants, but now technological advances have taken over many of these jobs. Likewise, the Internet has taken over many routine tasks from travel agents, stock brokers, and accountants. And, with high-speed data links, a lot of office work can be done more cheaply abroad.

What happens to the displaced workers? They move into other sectors of the economy as new jobs emerge. For example, by one estimate, about a quarter of today's labor force is in jobs that didn't even exist in 1967.

This emergence of new jobs and workers' ability to move into them are the hallmarks of a flexible economy—that is, an economy in which labor and capital resources move freely among firms and industries. And such flexibility is a significant strength of the U.S. economy. We operate in competitive markets, and competition, whether from domestic or foreign competitors, induces change. To adapt to that change, and to ease the burden of adjusting to it, flexible labor and capital markets are critically important.

## What Can Policies Do to Help U.S. Workers?

In terms of the overall economy, appropriate monetary and fiscal policies can ensure that aggregate demand keeps the economy on a sound footing, which helps generate jobs to replace those that have been lost.

But words about aggregate demand can seem like cold comfort to the individual workers whose offices and plants are closing because their jobs are going overseas. And concern for these workers, of course, is why there's interest in trying to restrict trade with tariffs, quotas, or other barriers. Indeed, such measures may actually succeed in slowing job losses in affected industries temporarily. But, as I hope I've illustrated, in the end, they impose significant costs on the rest of the economy that are much higher than any benefits.

---

*[Worker assistance policies should] help workers get through the hard times and help workers become more flexible.*

---

That's why I believe it's far more appropriate to have policies that focus on protecting the people at risk, not the jobs. Such policies should aim to do two things during difficult transitions: help workers get through the hard times and help workers become more flexible so they can adapt when they do face these kinds of changes. In fact, we have policies like these—unemployment insurance, for example. We even have policies specifically for manufacturing workers who have lost jobs to foreign competition. These trade-adjustment assistance programs offer both financial support for a time and the opportunity for training, so that workers can retool their skills and find new jobs. So, in order to help the service workers who have lost their jobs because of outsourcing, it might be appropriate to extend these programs to them.

I realize there's some debate about how effective the programs are, but the concepts they're built on are, to my mind, right on target—giving workers a safety net and giving workers the training and tools to qualify for the jobs being created in the U.S. In fact, such programs also could be appropriate for workers who have lost jobs in the wake of the technology-driven productivity surge.

In the long-run, of course, the solution is simple to state, but difficult—and costly—to implement. And that solution is improving the performance of the U.S. education system. Education is the bedrock of our current edge in technology and productivity. It's the key to producing workers with the flexibility to learn new skills as market conditions evolve. And it's the hope and promise we must provide for future generations of Americans.

# Job Losses from Globalization Are Exaggerated

*Paul Swaim and Raymond Torres*

**About the authors***: Paul Swaim and Raymond Torres are employed by the Directorate for Employment, Labour and Social Affairs, part of the Organisation for Economic Cooperation and Development (OECD), an organization of thirty countries that are committed to advancing democratic governments and market economies.*

Not long ago the term globalisation was held high as a positive force, a rallying cry for nations of all shapes and sizes to come together to build a safer, cleaner, more prosperous world. Today, to many, it is a byword for all things negative, not least for the "delocalisation" (or relocation) of jobs to low-wage countries. Take the debates over EU [European Union] enlargement and increased trade with China and India. There are diverse concerns animating these discussions, but the impact of globalisation on jobs is one that commentators and ordinary people keep repeating.

Whether globalisation is good or bad is an endless and distracting debate, but the bottom line is that policymakers certainly face a challenge. As for employment policy, three concrete questions matter: Does globalisation really cause job losses? If so, to what extent? And how can we respond?

## Job Losses Are Exaggerated

In so far as globalisation can be represented by international trade and foreign direct investment (FDI), the first answer is

Paul Swaim and Raymond Torres, "Jobs and Globalisation: Towards Policies That Work: While the Size of the Impact of Globalisation on Job Losses Is Often Exaggerated, There Is an Impact Nonetheless. How Must Public Policy Respond?" *OECD Observer*, No. 250, July 2005, pp. 11–13. Copyright © 2005, www.oecdobserver.org. OECD Publications and Information Centre. Reproduced by permission.

41

yes, some jobs in OECD [Organization for Economic Cooperation, a group of 30 countries that promotes free markets] countries (particularly in the manufacturing sector) are lost because of growing international competition, offshoring or other pressures generated by the international marketplace. But the answer to the second question is also important: the proportion of job losses caused by globalisation per se is far lower than many claim. Data from North America and Europe suggest between 4–17% of job displacements or layoffs are caused by international trade and investment. Other culprits include outdated technology, capital or skills, or just plain bad business management. Moreover, the other side of the ledger includes the fact that growing international trade and investment are associated with a sharp rise in overall living standards, not a fall. And globalization is also associated with many business opportunities and the creation of new jobs.

These observations should guide the public policy response, both to trade openness generally and to jobs and unemployment in particular. That is not to belittle the very real public concern that surrounds layoffs. When a firm relocates abroad, for those left behind it is a dislocation. Losing a job can be traumatic, and the very prospect of change can cause anxiety and disruption in the lives of individuals, families and whole communities. Even if a displaced worker finds a new job, the transition remains an ordeal that must be managed.

In other words, while the true impact of globalisation on job losses is often exaggerated, there is a real impact nonetheless, and so public policy is needed to enhance the capacity of the market to enable adjustment. Indeed, when displacement results from deliberate policy decisions to liberalise trade and investment flows, like removing tariffs, policy measures to manage adjustment become a duty of good governance. The number of job displacements may be less than some claim, but the policy difficulties should not be underestimated.

## What Can Governments Do?

The first thing is to accept that protection for certain vulnerable industries is not an option—that would be like building castles in the sand and would simply postpone possibly more painful, costly adjustment later on. Consider those displacement rates again. While white-collar jobs are also affected by international trade. and investment, especially in business services and IT [information technology], trade-related job losses are proportionately higher in manufacturing than in the services sector. In general, most job losses that are associated with trade/FDI are in areas where comparative advantage is slipping, as in cars or textiles, and where skills are becoming obsolete because of technological change, ageing, productivity, and so on. They mainly affect less skilled workers, who find it particularly hard to find a new job. When they do find one, they may have to take sizeable pay cuts.

---

*Displaced US manufacturing workers experience an average pay cut of 13% once re-employed, with a quarter experiencing earnings losses of 30% or more.*

---

Understanding these trends helps us to shift the debate from one about the pros and cons of globalisation, to a pragmatic debate on how to build policies to assist displaced workers more effectively to find new and better jobs.

The policy implications of trade-related job losses vary according to factors such as the length of time people spend out of work, earnings losses in new jobs, and so on. In the United States, 63% of workers who lose their jobs in high-international-competition manufacturing industries are re-employed within about two years, somewhat lower than the 69% rate for the service sector. Reemployment rates are lower in Europe, averaging 57% overall and just 52% in high-international-competition industries within manufacturing.

As for wages, displaced US manufacturing workers experience an average pay cut of 13% once re-employed, with a quarter experiencing earnings losses of 30% or more. In the services sector, the average loss is just 4%. Earnings losses in the new job tend to be smaller in Europe, although finding that job is more difficult than in the US.

Why do workers who lose their jobs in industries facing intense import competition fare somewhat worse than other job losers? Globalisation appears not to be the cause of that. Rather, compared with others, in both Europe and the US, this group tends to be older, less educated and have held down the lost job for longer, characteristics that are associated with above-average re-employment difficulties and larger earnings losses following re-employment. Nevertheless, globalisation may have contributed to the original job loss, and this demands a policy response.

Active labour market programmes, unemployment benefits and other direct measures normally associated with job loss are therefore vital. On top of that, indirect measures are needed to provide an economic environment where workers from declining sectors can find new jobs that make good use of their skills. The overarching need here is for general policies that strengthen job creation, upgrade work force skills and steer workers towards the jobs where they are most productive. . . .

Assistance to trade-displaced workers can be incorporated into an overall strategy for achieving high employment rates in the context of continuous structural economic change. While there may be various ways of achieving this, the key message remains the same: open markets result in some dislocation in labour markets and policy measures must be put in place that compensate job losers while promoting their re-employment chances. In a sense, workers will accept to swim with globalisation, as long as the policies are there to ensure they do not sink because of it.

CHAPTER 2

# Does Globalization Harm
Developing Countries?

# Chapter Preface

Much of the backlash against globalization has come from developing countries, many of which claim that liberal trade policies have brought them only greater poverty and pain. While some developing nations, such as China and India, seem to have prospered greatly from opening their markets and expanding their trade, other less developed areas that have tried to follow the free trade prescription for economic development are sinking deeper and deeper into economic stagnation and instability.

Africa appears to be one of globalization's biggest failures. Despite the adoption of policies advocated by international free trade organizations, such as the World Trade Organization (WTO) and the International Monetary Fund (IMF), the African region continues to be one of the poorest and most desperate regions in the world today. Although rich in valuable natural resources such as diamonds, minerals, and oil, many African countries have not been able to create economic development and remain victimized by widespread, heartbreaking poverty and malnutrition. This poverty, and a resulting lack of adequate health care, has produced the world's largest AIDS epidemic. In 2005, according to the United Nations, Sub-Saharan Africa recorded 25.8 million people (out of 40 million worldwide) living with the disease, and that same year, 2.4 million Africans died of AIDS (out of 3.1 million deaths worldwide). Many of Africa's countries, too, are embroiled in wars, violent ethnic conflicts, and cross-border skirmishes that result in a seemingly endless cycle of brutal deaths, rapes, and maimings.

Many of these conditions are rooted in Africa's history of colonialism and incompetent local leadership, but a growing number of experts today agree that expanded trade brought by globalization has only exacerbated Africa's problems. As

Nigerian journalist Sunday Dare argued in a 2001 article in *Dollars and Sense* magazine:

> The expansion of corporate dominance [in Africa] has accentuated the steady descent into near economic strangulation and political chaos. Many transnational corporations (TNCs) have acted as economic predators in Africa, gobbling up national resources, distorting national economic policies, exploiting and changing labor relations, committing environmental despoliation, violating sovereignties, and manipulating governments and the media. In order to ensure uninterrupted access to resources, TNCs have also supported repressive African leaders, warlords, and guerrilla fighters, thus serving as catalysts for lethal conflict and impeding prospects for development and peace.

Even African countries deemed by many to be free trade successes, such as the nation of South Africa, suffer negative effects from global economic policies. In 1994, following decades of British colonialism and repressive apartheid, Nelson Mandela was elected that country's first black leader amid great fanfare and optimism. Many South Africans hoped that their country, under this new leadership, would become a beacon for democracy, multiracialism, and prosperity. Even before Mandela was elected, however, the South African government adopted liberal trade and economic policies recommended by the IMF in exchange for a $750 million loan. Once elected, Nelson Mandela and his new government enthusiastically embraced the IMF program, as did the country's next president, Thabo Mbeki, elected in 1999.

The IMF policies emphasized cutting government spending, reducing government taxing of corporate profits, and privatizing South Africa's public companies and services. They also opened the country's national currency to international markets and imposed drastic reductions on tariffs that had been designed to protect South Africa's key economic sectors, such as textiles and agricultural goods. As the investment climate improved, large transnational corporations moved into the country to develop its natural resources, such as gold and other minerals.

Instead of bringing prosperity, however, the free trade agenda produced only anemic economic growth. South Africa's annual gross domestic product (GDP), a measure of its total economic output, has remained stagnant at about 1 to 3 percent since the early 1990s. Although corporate investors and some elites have fared well, this economic situation has left about half of the population entrenched in poverty, caused chronic unemployment as high as 40 or 50 percent, and resulted in massive cuts in government social services and health care and cutoffs of basic services such as electricity and water. South Africa also has more people living with HIV/AIDS than any other country in the world. These conditions have sparked bitter citizen protests, and the ruling African National Congress (ANC) has responded, in turn, by teargassing and arresting demonstrators, becoming increasingly repressive. Many people fear that the country is regressing to the time of the old, apartheid South Africa, except that today the purpose is to suppress opposition to the government's economic policies.

In recent years, South Africa and other African countries have begun to object to what they view as the unfair aspects of globalization. In particular, poor countries have criticized global free trade policies that often have required undeveloped economies to lower tariffs and other trade barriers, and open to the vagaries of international competition, while allowing many industrial countries to maintain their own trade barriers. The United States and the European Union, for example, have kept government subsidies and trade protections for many of their agricultural products, from corn to cotton, but have pushed for developing nations to lower agricultural tariffs. This situation has given multinational corporations access to many of the raw materials produced by developing nations, such as Africa's oil and minerals, but prevented those same developing nations from competing fairly with products produced by rich, industrialized countries. As South Africa's President Thabo Mbeki put it in 2004, "We ask for equitable access to the world's markets."

This question of whether globalization is inherently biased in favor of richer, more developed countries—and against poorer, undeveloped nations—lies at the heart of the controversy reflected of the viewpoints in the following chapter.

# Unregulated Globalization Can Lead to Impoverishment for Developing Countries

*Lucky O. Imade*

**About the author***: Lucky O. Imade is an assistant professor of international relations at Shaw University, in Raleigh, North Carolina.*

Globalization is certainly the buzzword of the new millennium. The nature and impact of globalization has been the subject of profound debate and concern in economic circles since the mid-1990s. The controversy surrounding the on-going debates about globalization is whether unfettered market forces will further diverge or converge income the world over. On the one hand, proponents of globalization say it has promoted information exchange, led to a greater understanding of other cultures, raised living standards, increased purchasing power (most especially in the west) and allowed democracy to triumph over communism. On the other hand, opponents of globalization, such as those who protested against the ministerial meetings of the World Trade Organization (WTO) in Seattle and most recently in Quebec City, say the West's gain is at the expense of developing countries. These opponents charge that globalization is synonymous with imperialism and does little more than encourage corporations to relocate factories to countries with the cheapest labor and the weakest environmental laws. They further argue that, "even in the developed world, not everyone has been a winner. The freedoms granted by globalization are leading to increased insecurity in the workplace. Unskilled workers in particular are under threat as companies shift their production lines overseas to low-wage economies."

## Impoverishment and Prosperity

Mainstream economic thought promises that globalization would lift the poor above poverty, dissolve dictatorships, protect the environment, integrate cultures, and most importantly, reverse the growing economic gap between rich and poor countries of the world. . . .

[However,] a large percentage of the world's population feels excluded from the benefits of globalization. Statistics abound showing how globalization is increasingly polarizing the world into two different camps—impoverishment and prosperity. As the juxtaposition of wealth and poverty at the opposite extremes of the globe continues, thus the orthodox model of development is being held up for closer scrutiny, as we become knowledgeable of the challenges and opportunities that globalization . . . [brings]. Given all the uncertainties about globalization, the time is right to rethink the nature of North-South [referring to developed-undeveloped regions of the world] economic relations in the global economy. Is the relationship based on a "win-win" situation? Finding the answer requires going beyond the modernization thesis and employing an approach based on four related and overlapping, but still distinct concepts: technological innovation and information revolution, trade liberalization, internationalization of capital, and the new international division of labor.

## Explaining the Gap in Prosperity

These four concepts are the basic building blocks for explaining the two faces of globalization—while some countries are enjoying the prosperity globalization brings in its wake, others are languishing in impoverishment as a result of globalization. The level of technological innovation and information revolution in one's country determines whether a country reaps the benefits of globalization or not. The more a country liberalizes its economy and at the same time the more safety valves it creates to protect certain industries determines how competitive that country will be in the international market. Internationalization of capital—the more production and capital are concentrated in few countries (mostly advanced industrialized countries), the more it engenders monopolistic practices and stifles competition; and the new international division of labor—the more some countries specialize in the production of primary products while others specialize in manufactured goods, the more the gap between rich and poor countries will continue to widen.

The degree of technological innovation and information revolution taking place in a country determines the benefits of globalization accruing to the country concerned. Moreover, an expanding high-tech, information-based economy increasingly defines globalization and shapes the business cycles within it. The size of a nation economy protects a nation's market from trade liberalization. The internationalization of capital favors the rich and well-endowed nations more than the poor ones, and moreover, links more countries to a worldwide division of labor and diminishes autonomous development, thus leading to intensification of the contradictions inherent in capitalism. Much of the flow of capital, labor, service, and goods among Asia, America, and Europe is technology-based. The benefits of the new international division of labor [are different for] . . . different countries. These concepts help us make sense of what globalization means and which country is well positioned to reap its benefits and which ones will fall behind.

---

*For globalization to become a win-win situation, rules, regulations, and international conventions must count as much as market mechanisms.*

---

The ways in which these ideas fit together helps illuminate such crucial globalization issues as the relationship between impoverishment and prosperity, environmental degradation, national cultures and identities, cultural imperialism, global economies of scale, digital divide, mono-cropping, cheap labor, and the interactions among individuals, firms, and governments. These concepts serve as powerful tools for analysis, not as isolated variables but as patterns of interrelationships. . . .

## The Need for International Regulation

For globalization to become a win-win situation, rules, regulations, and international conventions must count as much as market mechanism[s]. The way these four concepts—technological innovation, trade liberalization, internationalization of capital, and the new international economic order—interact, shows that without an effective international rules and legal system that protects labor, environment, and monopolistic practices, globalization can lead to oppression, exploitation, and impoverishment. The fact remains: capitalism has always operated within the context of the rule of law.

---

*Unbridled globalization—technological innovation, trade liberalization, internationalization of capital, and the new international division of labor—could wreak havoc on some countries.*

---

In trying to explain why globalization is not a win-win game, we must ask fundamental questions in terms of these four concepts: Is the information revolution beneficial to all or to some well-endowed countries? Is trade liberalization really a free trade or there are some elements of protectionism acting as a stumbling block on the way of some countries? Does internationalization of capital add up to monopoly capital, which might stifle competition or does it allow infant industries from the South to compete fairly? Does the new international division of labor engender comparative disadvantage or will it relegate the weak economy to the periphery merely as supplier of raw materials, cheap labor, and market for finished products? These questions relate to how unbridled globalization—technological innovation, trade liberalization, internationalization of capital, and the new international division of labor—could wreak havoc on some countries while simultaneously opening the doors of opportunity to others. . . .

If there is any lesson to be drawn from the events of September 11, 2001, it is that "while many in the first world benefit from free markets in capital, labor, and goods, these same anarchic markets leave ordinary people in the third world largely unprotected." Because we have become a society glutted on market fundamentalism, laissez faire, and affluence, regulation of the market is being nonchalantly shoved aside. Because we have lost a proper perspective of time, history, and education, Third World development is taking its dying breaths. Even if Third World were the only victim, it would still be a remarkable tragedy in the annals of Western civilization. But what is worse is that all these ills that plague Third World nations reveal deeper problems about the West, most especially the United States and the disastrous direction it is headed. What has become apparent to the rest of us after September 11 is that that same deregulated disorder from which financial and trade institutions imagine they benefit is the very disorder on which terrorism depends. . . .

## A Global New Deal

The global economy today is analogous to the U.S. economy during the Great Depression of 1930s. The Great Depression economy was characterized by slow economic growth, income inequalities, and high rate of unemployment. The president in the White House at the time of the Great Depression was Herbert Hoover. A Republican who did not believe in government interference with the market, he folded his arms and watched the U.S. economy collapse. The consequences of such inaction kept the nation in economic malaise for a long period of time. It took the genius of Franklin D. Roosevelt's New Deal legislation to put the economic back on track. The question that comes to mind now is: Will this strategy work in the international arena, where there is no central authority to sanction its implementation?

---

*There is a broad consensus among opponents of globalization . . . that completely free unregulated capitalist growth is not likely to address poverty.*

---

There is a broad consensus among opponents of globalization who sought [an] alternative approach that completely free unregulated capitalist growth is not likely to address poverty and that some deliberate measure[s] are needed—by governments and international institutions—to facilitate the inclusion of poor countries and people. . . . [A Global New Deal would be a step in the right direction and would include:]

1. Creation of an integrated program for commodities (IPC), to stockpile and control the price of commodities during periods of oversupply and scarcity.

2. Extension and liberalization of Generalized System of Preferences (GSPs) in collaboration with the execution of WTO [World Trade Organization] Doha Development Agenda—in which rich nations promise the reduction of their trade barriers.

3. Development of [a] debt-relief program.

4. Increasing Official Development Assistance (ODA) from rich, developed nations of the North to the less developed South.

5. Changing the decision-making process in major international institutions such as the United Nations, IMF [International Monetary Fund], World Bank, and WTO to give more voice to Southern nations and reduce developed nations' control of these institutions.

6. Increasing the economic sovereignty of LDCs [Less Developed Countries]. Several initiatives were stipulated under this umbrella. Key among them were: ensuring LDCs' greater control over their natural resources; increased access to Western technology; the ability to regulate MNCs [Multi-national Corporations]; and preferential trade policies that would stabilize prices for commodities from LDCs and ensure these countries greater access to developed countries' markets.

7. Tackling greenhouse gases—There is broad agreement among scientists that human activity is leading to potentially disastrous global warming, and that these changes in climate will be especially burdensome for poor countries and poor people. The report urges more effective international cooperation to address these problems.

Fair competition is a buzzword when the playing field is not leveled. Accepting these modifications to the global economy will to some extent level that playing field. Failure to implement this Global New Deal will once again throw the international economy system into disarray, and bailing it out will be more costly than fixing it. In the words of [economist] Dani Rodrik, "'Winners' have as much at stake from the possible consequences of social instability as the 'losers'. Social disintegration is not a spectator sport—those on the sidelines also get splashed with mud from the field. Ultimately, the deepening of social fissures can harm all."

---

*[A] Global New Deal ... will breathe new life into most of the world's ailing economies if allowed to work properly by the developed world.*

---

It is obvious that a Marshall plan for Third World nations after slavery and colonialism could have gone a long way to revamp their economies. Instead, developing countries were dragged into the world economy in what [economist] Paul Baran described as ... the "Prussian way"—not through the growth of small, competitive enterprise, but through the transfer from abroad of advanced, monopolistic business.

Developing countries can make a vital contribution through effective domestic policies in conjunction with international efforts to ensure sustainable growth and development:

- Improving the investment climate in developing countries—Encouraging investment and creating jobs requires good economic governance—measures to combat corruption, better-functioning bureaucracies and better regulation, contract enforcement, providing social protection to a changing labor market, and protection of property rights;

- Structural reform to encourage domestic competition;

- Improving delivery of education and health services— The developing countries that have gained the most from integrating into the world economy have shown impressive gains in primary education and infant mortality.

This Global New Deal, according to its proponent[s,] will breathe new life into most of the world's ailing economies if allowed to work properly by the developed world.

# Globalization Reforms Have Slowed Economic Growth for Most Poor Countries

*Mark Weisbrot, Dean Baker, and David Rosnick*

**About the authors**: *Mark Weisbrot and Dean Baker are econo-mists and co-directors of the Center for Economic and Policy Re-search (CEPR), a privately-funded research and public informa-tion organization that focuses on social and economic issues. David Rosnick is a research associate with CEPR.*

Over the past 25 years a number of economic reforms have taken place in low- and middle-income countries. These reforms, as a group, have been given various labels: "liberalization," "globalization," or "free-market" are among the most common descriptions. Among the reforms widely implemented have been the reduction of restrictions on inter-national trade and capital flows, large-scale privatizations of state-owned enterprises, tighter fiscal and monetary policies (higher interest rates), labor market reforms, and increasing accumulation of foreign reserve holdings. Many of these re-forms have been implemented with the active support of mul-tilateral lending institutions such as the International Mon-etary Fund and the World Bank, as well as the G-7 [Group of 7, the seven most industrialized countries] governments, and have often been required in order for countries to have access to credit from these and other sources. But regardless of ori-gin, labels or political perspectives, there is a general consen-sus that the majority of developing countries have benefited economically from the reforms, even if they have sometimes been accompanied by increasing inequality or other unin-tended consequences.

Mark Weisbrot, Dean Baker, and David Rosnick, "The Scorecard on Development: 25 Years of Diminished Progress," Center for Economic and Policy Research, September 2005. www.cepr.net/publications/development_2005_09.pdf.

# Slower Economic Growth for Developing Countries

This paper looks at the available data on economic growth and various social indicators—including health outcomes and education—and finds that, contrary to popular belief, the past 25 years have seen a sharply slower rate of economic growth and reduced progress on social indicators for the vast majority of low and middle-income countries. Of course it is still possible that some or even all of the policy reforms of the past 25 years have had net positive effects, or that they will have such an impact at some point in the future. But the fact that these effects have not yet shown up in the data, for developing countries as a group—and that in fact the data show a marked decline in progress over the last quarter-century—is very significant. If the data and trends presented below were well known, it would very likely have an impact on policy discussions and research. Most importantly, there would be a much greater interest in finding out what has gone wrong over the last 25 years.

In order to evaluate the progress of the last 25 years, it is necessary to have a benchmark for comparison. In other words, for the world as a whole, there is almost always economic growth, technological progress, and therefore social progress over time. The relevant question is not whether there has been income growth and social progress, but the rate of such progress as compared with what has been feasible in the past.

For this paper, we have chosen to compare the past 25 years (1980–2005) with the previous 20 years: 1960–1980. This is a fair comparison. While the 1960s were a period of exceptional economic performance, the 1970s suffered from two major oil shocks that led to worldwide recessions: in 1974–75, and again at the end of the decade. The seventies were also a period of high inflation in both developing and developed countries. So this twenty-year period is not a particularly high benchmark for comparison with the most recent 25 years. If the 1950s were included, it would have made the benchmark for comparison higher, since the 1950s were generally a period of good growth for the developing world. But there is not much good data for the 1950s; and many of the developing countries did not become independent until the late 1950s or 1960s. . . .

---

*There is a sharp slowdown in the rate of growth of per capita income for the vast majority of low- and middle-income countries.*

---

## A Slowdown in GDP Growth

The growth of income (or GDP) per person is the most basic measure of economic progress that economists use. . . .

There is a sharp slowdown in the rate of growth of per capita income for the vast majority of low- and middle-income countries. This is probably the most important economic change that has taken place in the world during the last quarter century. It is much more difficult to reduce poverty or inequality in the face of such a growth slowdown. When a country's economy is growing, it is at least possible for the poor to share equally or even disproportionately in the gains from productivity growth. When there is very little growth in income per person, such improvements are much harder to achieve, and may be politically impossible to the extent that poverty alleviation depends on actually reducing the current income of the middle and upper classes.

One region that has been particularly affected by this growth slowdown has been Latin America. Income per capita for the region grew by more than 80 percent from 1960–1979, but only about 11 percent from 1980–2000 and 3 percent for 2000–2005. This has been a drastic change. If Brazil, for example, had continued to grow at its pre-1980 rate, the country would have European living standards today. Mexico would not be far behind. Instead, the region has suffered its worst 25-year economic performance in modern Latin American history, even including the years of the Great Depression. . . .

## Reduced Progress in Health and Education

As would be expected in a period of sharply reduced economic growth, the last 25 years also shows slower progress on health outcomes. . . . There is a noticeable slowdown [in life expectancy] in all groups except the highest quintile [category], which contains countries where life expectancy is between 69 and 76 years. The biggest drop was in the fourth quintile, with life expectancy between 44 and 53. These countries saw an average annual increase of 0.56 years for 1960–1980, but almost no progress—0.03 percent for the second period. . . .

A significant part of this story is Sub-Saharan Africa, which dominates the bottom two quintiles for the 1980–2005 period, and has some impact on the middle quintile. However, even if all the Sub-Saharan African countries are removed from the data, there is still a decline in progress for the bottom three quintiles, with no change for the second. So the decline in progress on life expectancy occurs across a broad range of low- and middle-income countries, and is not confined to any particular region. . . .

*Some economists have recently concluded that more "policy autonomy" . . . is needed for developing countries.*

Given the sharp slowdown in economic growth, it would not be surprising to find that public spending on education did not increase as much in the second period as in the first, and that is indeed the case. . . .

Summing up the data on education, most low- and middle-income countries made less progress since 1980 in increasing enrollment at the primary and secondary levels of education, as compared with the prior period (1960–1980). This was not true for tertiary education. Public spending on education also increased at a slower rate in the second period, and the rate of progress on literacy also slowed. This—together with the slowdown in economic growth—could explain the reduced progress for low- and middle-income countries on the educational front. The changes in measures of educational progress are not as pronounced as indicators of health outcomes, or of economic growth, but they are overwhelmingly in the same direction, showing reduced progress since 1980. . . .

## What Went Wrong?

It is generally difficult to show a clear relationship between any particular policy change and economic outcomes, especially across countries. There are many changes that take place at the same time, and causality is difficult to establish. It is certainly possible that the decline in economic and social progress that has taken place over the last 25 years would have been even worse in the absence of the policy changes that were adopted [to encourage globalization]. But that remains to be demonstrated.

In the meantime, a long-term failure of the type documented here should at the very least shift the burden of proof to those who maintain that the major policy changes of the last 25 years have raised living standards in the majority of developing countries, and encourage skepticism with regard to economists or institutions who believe they have found a formula for economic growth and development. Indeed, some economists have recently concluded that more "policy autonomy"—the ability of countries to make their own decisions about economic policy—is needed for developing countries. Most importantly, the outcome of the last 25 years should have economists and policy-makers thinking about what has gone wrong.

# The Concerns of Developing Countries Are Not Being Addressed by Global Trade Talks

*Michael Fleshman*

**About the author***: Michael Fleshman is the human rights coordinator for the Africa Fund, a U.S. organization that works to influence U.S. foreign policy to benefit Africa.*

After six days of arm-twisting, all-night bargaining sessions and closed-door meetings in Hong Kong, an eleventh-hour concession by Europe on farm subsidies saved the December 2005 summit meeting of the World Trade Organization (WTO) from another embarrassing collapse. The European move kept the troubled global trade liberalization talks, launched at Doha, Qatar, in 2001, alive—but just barely.... Four years after the industrial North [referring to developed countries] promised that Doha's central purpose would be to aid the world's poor, many African and other developing countries are beginning to question not just the outcome in Hong Kong but the fairness of the global trading system itself....

## Doha Trade Talks Geared to Developing Countries

The decision to label the Doha process a "development" round [of trade talks] reflected the new assertiveness of poor countries at the WTO. The trade group's 1999 meeting in Seattle ended in failure in part because developing countries, led by Africa, refused to launch talks on new issues until inequities

Michael Fleshman, "Trade Talks: Where Is the Development?" *Africa Renewal, United Nations,* April 2006, vol. 20, iss. 1, p. 14. www.un.org/ecosocdev/geninfo/afrec/vol20no1 /201-trade-talks.html.

in the previous trade agreement, known as the Uruguay Round, were fixed. To secure consent on talks in areas of concern to them, developed countries agreed in Doha to include a number of "development" issues of particular concern to Africa, including:

- Correcting the inequities of previous trade agreements

- Eliminating Northern [referring to northern developed countries] agricultural subsidies, totalling some $350 bn [billion] annually, which depress world prices and bring unfair competition with unsubsidized African produce

- Strengthening "special and differential treatment" provisions that allow flexibility in how poor countries adjust to WTO agreements

- Improving access by developing countries to consumers in rich countries, including duty-free access for the exports of the 50 nations designated as "least developed countries" (LDCs), 33 of which are in Africa

- Expanding "aid for trade" to help African countries produce more for export, improve skills and efficiency in trade-related institutions and defray the cost of complying with WTO rules.The absence of progress on this "Doha Development Agenda" led to the collapse of the 2003 WTO summit in Cancún, Mexico, when frustrated developing countries again rejected new talks. Continued deadlock in the vital negotiations over agricultural subsidies and inaction on most other development issues seemed likely to doom the Hong Kong meeting as well. . . .

## The Hong Kong Doha Talks in 2005

The last-minute announcement . . . that the EU would eliminate farm-export subsidies by 2013, combined with acceptance of a package of modest benefits for the LDCs, promises of increased funding for "aid for trade" and limited moves by Washington to address the particular demands of West African farmers injured by US cotton subsidies, was enough to salvage the negotiations. In return, African and other poor developing countries agreed to expanded talks over liberalization of services, a longstanding European and US objective. . . .

Nevertheless, a number of analysts in both the North and the South argue that, in virtually every sector, Hong Kong was a setback for Africa's development goals and a betrayal of the promise of the Doha agenda.

In agriculture, trade expert Aileen Kwa . . . [explained], "developed countries really didn't do anything on their subsidies besides making much of the European end date" of 2013. . . . The same is true of US farm subsidies, she asserted. . . . The deal on industrial tariffs is no better. At the Hong Kong summit, developing countries reluctantly agreed to a formula for reductions that could require poor countries to cut levies on manufactured goods more rapidly than wealthy states. African trade ministers argued that structural adjustment programmes and bilateral aid agreements outside the WTO framework have already forced deep reductions in their tariffs and that further cuts are both unfair and unwise. . . .

---

*The sceptics' arguments have been strengthened by the failure of the global trading system to deliver prosperity and economic development for the African poor.*

---

An agreement to give duty- and quota-free access to 97 per cent of LDC exports to Northern markets was hailed as a major breakthrough at Hong Kong. But even that, critics say, is more symbolism than substance. The offer sounds good . . . but even 100 per cent duty-free access for LDC exports counts for little if countries have little to trade. Although about one in eight of the world's people live in a least developed country, the economies of those countries typically produce few products for trade and account for barely half a per cent of global exports. . . .

African countries also failed to make headway in efforts to correct damaging inequities and imbalances in existing trade rules. . . . African demands for "special and differential" treatment (S&D) provisions—intended to give poor countries greater flexibility in applying WTO rules—fared no better. . . . On balance, said Ambassador [Samuel] Amehou [of the West African republic of Benin] about Hong Kong, "the final results were really below our expectations. We were expecting more in agriculture, on LDCs and S&D. But we only got small progress in export subsidies, small progress for the LDCs and nothing special on implementation issues." . . .

## Doha Trade Talks Unlikely to Benefit Poor Countries

The sceptics' arguments have been strengthened by the failure of the global trading system to deliver prosperity and economic development for the African poor. By most measures, Africa is poorer, less industrialized and less of a contributor to world trade than in 1986, when the launch of trade talks in Uruguay marked the beginning of the modern era of trade liberalization. Twenty years later, new research by the World Bank has led some economists to conclude that Africa may have failed to reap the promised benefits of free trade because they were never really there.

In 2003, a study by the World Bank predicted that successful completion of the Doha talks would generate a staggering $832 bn [billion] of new wealth by 2015, with most of that amount, $539 bn, going to developing countries—enough to lift 144 million people out of poverty. The figures were widely cited by trade negotiators, journalists, anti-poverty advocates and senior UN officials in urging poor countries to liberalize more quickly.

More recent research, however, casts grave doubts on the earlier, rosy estimates and raises new questions about the value of trade liberalization as a development tool for poor countries. In advance of the Hong Kong meeting the World Bank reported that, under ideal conditions, including such unlikely developments as the elimination of all tariffs and agricultural subsidies and full global employment, Doha would generate $287 bn in new wealth by 2015—just a third of the 2003 estimate. Under this admittedly unrealistic model, developing countries would gain just $90 bn, or 31 per cent of the benefits, with the balance going to wealthy countries.

---

*The LDCs [least developed countries], with the smallest and weakest economies, would likely benefit the least [from a Doha agreement].*

---

When more realistic assumptions are used, the same researchers concluded that Doha would produce only $96 bn in total gains—with $80 bn flowing to the industrialized North and just $16 bn to the developing South.

Far from Africa being able to "trade its way out of poverty," a detailed analysis of the World Bank report by two US researchers, Timothy Wise of Tufts University and Boston University Professor Kevin P. Gallagher, found that the Bank's "realistic" analysis of a Doha agreement would increase the average income of each citizen in a developing country by less than one US cent per day and reduce the global poverty rate by less than half a percent. "Hardly a good advertisement for this so-called 'development round' of global trade talks," they observed.

Moreover, half of the expected gains, some $8 bn, would go to only eight countries: Argentina, Brazil, China, India, Mexico, Thailand, Turkey and Vietnam. The LDCs, with the smallest and weakest economies, would likely benefit the least. The costs and losses associated with continued liberalization are spread more widely, however. Wise and Gallagher, citing additional World Bank studies, estimated that the administrative cost of complying with WTO-mandated requirements in just three areas—food sanitation, intellectual property and customs reforms—would average $130 mn per year for each poor country, for a global total of some $4.4 bn.

Deep cuts in tariffs could also prove costly for African and other developing countries. According to the UN Conference on Trade and Development (UNCTAD), tariffs generate about 20 per cent of government revenue in developing countries. That figure is far higher than in developed countries and represents a vital source of funding for health, education, infrastructure and other development programmes. Depending on the final outcome of negotiations on tariff reductions, UNCTAD estimates that revenue losses in poor countries could reach $60 bn. . . .

## Does Globalization Hurt the Poor?

The failure of trade liberalization to deliver on its development promises is leading a growing number of economists to question whether trade liberalization helps or hurts the poor. Dr. Thomas Palley, an economist at Yale University, wrote in early 2006: "Mainstream policy economics has been gradually lowering its claims about the positive impact of trade on development and poverty reduction. . . . A decade ago, mainstream policy economics argued vigorously that trade promotes development. If this were true, given the massive increase in global trade over the last 25 years, the global economy ought to have experienced accelerated growth. Instead, global economic growth has actually slowed relative to the prior quarter-century. This suggests that trade is at best only weakly associated with growth" and even more weakly with poverty reduction. . . . Arguing that poor countries should consider abandoning free-trade development models in favour of protecting and developing their domestic markets, Dr. Palley cited recent research to conclude that expanded trade is a result of development, rather than a cause of development.

The World Bank's former senior economist, Nobel Laureate Joseph Stiglitz, is also questioning the link between development and free trade. "As chief economist of the World Bank, I reviewed the Uruguay Round of 1994 and concluded that both its agenda and outcomes discriminated against developing countries," he wrote in December 2005. . . . In an essay entitled "Fair Trade for None," he noted, "Unsurprisingly the rich countries' negotiators throw around big numbers when describing the gains from even an imperfect agreement. But they did the same thing last time, too. Developing countries soon discovered that their gains were far less than advertised, and the poorest countries found to their dismay that they were actually worse off."

With negotiations to complete the Doha round looming, the economist cautioned, "Will the benefits—increased access to international markets—be greater than the costs of meeting rich countries' demands? Many developing countries are likely to come to the conclusion that no agreement is better than a bad agreement, particularly one as unfair as the last."

# Multinational Corporations Do Not Exploit Poor Countries

*Jagdish Bhagwati*

**About the author**: *Jagdish Bhagwati is an economist at Columbia University and a recognized expert on international trade. This article is adapted from his latest book,* In Defense of Globalization *(2004).*

There is a fierce debate today between those who consider globalization to be a malign influence on poor nations and those who find it a positive force. This debate focuses not just on trade, but also on multinational corporations. The hard evidence strongly suggests that the positive view is more realistic. There are many reasons to believe that multinationals in particular do good, not harm, in the developing world. [However,] if any conviction strongly unites the critics of multinationals today, it is that they exploit workers in poor countries. Ire has been aroused by the assumption that rich, deep-pocketed corporations pay "unfair" or "inadequate" wages overseas. More generally, companies are condemned for violating "labor rights."

## Multinational Corporations Do Not Pay Unfair Wages

The typical critique asserts that if a Liz Claiborne jacket sells for $190 in New York, while the female worker abroad who sews it gets only 60 cents an hour, that is obviously exploitation. But there is no necessary relationship between the price of a specific product and the wage paid by a company. For starters, for every jacket that sells, there may be nine that do

Jagdish Bhagwati, "Do Multinational Corporations Hurt Poor Countries?" *The American Enterprise*, June 2004, vol. 15, iss. 4, p. 28.

not. So the effective price of a jacket one must consider is a tenth of the sold jacket: $19, not $190. And distribution costs and tariff duties on apparel almost double the price of a jacket between the time it arrives at the dock or airport in New York and finds its way to a Lord & Taylor display.

---

*[Vietnamese] workers in foreign-owned enterprises generally make almost twice the salary of the average worker employed at a Vietnamese company.*

---

It is often assumed that multinationals earn huge monopoly profits while paying their workers minimal wages, and that these firms should therefore share their "excess" profit with their workers. But nearly all multinationals such as Liz Claiborne and Nike operate in fiercely competitive environments. A recent study of the profits performance of 214 companies in the 1999 Fortune Global 500 list showed a rather sorry achievement—about 8.3 percent profit on foreign assets. Where are the huge spoils to be shared with workers?

Let's look at the facts on wage payments. Good empirical studies have been conducted in Bangladesh, Mexico, Shanghai, Indonesia, Vietnam, and elsewhere. And these studies find that multinationals actually pay what economists call a "wage premium," that is, an average wage that exceeds the going rate in the area where they are located. Affiliates of some U.S. multinationals pay a premium over local wages that ranges from 40 to 100 percent.

In one careful and convincing study, the economist Paul Glewwe, using Vietnamese household data for 1997–98, was able to isolate the incomes of workers employed in foreign-owned firms, joint ventures, and Vietnamese-owned enterprises. About half the Vietnamese workers in the study worked in the foreign textile or leather firms that are so often criticized. Contrary to the steady refrain from the critics, Glewwe found that workers in foreign-owned enterprises generally make almost twice the salary of the average worker employed at a Vietnamese company. As Glewwe points out:

> The data also show that people who obtained employment in foreign-owned enterprises and joint ventures in Vietnam in the 1990s experienced increases in household income (as measured by per capita consumption expenditures) that exceeded the average increases for all Vietnamese households. This appears to contradict the claims that foreign-owned enterprises in poor countries such as Vietnam are "sweatshops." On the other hand, it is clear that the wages paid by these enterprises . . . are a fraction of wages paid in the U.S. and other wealthy countries. Yet Vietnam is so poor that it is better for a Vietnamese person to obtain this kind of employment than almost any other kind available in Vietnam.

## Multinationals Do Not Violate Labor Rights

But there remains the accusation that global corporations violate labor rights. Many damning charges are made, and anti-globalization activists are not beyond trumpeting the occasional lie, much like the corporations, politicians, and bureaucrats they excoriate. Only after IKEA was accused of exploitative child labor by its suppliers was it discovered that the German film documenting the abuse was simply faked by activists. . . .

Sometimes when critics of multinationals attack, it is not egregious violations of local laws that are at issue. It is rather the claim that the companies do not meet the demands of "decency," or Western norms, or perhaps international law. This route to condemning multinationals is quite problematic, however.

For one thing, developing-world regulations may be less demanding than international ones (just as American standards are often below those of Europe and even Canada) for good reasons. Take the case of working hours, which can be quite long in some poor countries. As Nicholas Kristof and

Sheryl WuDunn have pointed out in the *New York Times Magazine*, the young Third World workers who toil long hours at multinational factories generally do so voluntarily. Why? Because they want to make money as quickly as possible so they can return to their rural homes. Like many of us who work long hours, they are not being exploited, they drive themselves.

Kristof and WuDunn quote workers in a leather-stitching factory in the Chinese boomtown of Dongguan, who tell them they all regard it as a plus that the factory allows them to work long hours every day. Indeed, some had sought out this factory precisely because it offered them the chance to earn more. "It's actually pretty annoying how hard they want to work," said the factory manager, a Hong Kong man. "It means we have to worry about security and have a supervisor around almost constantly."

## Benefits of Multinational Investments

Not only are multinationals wrongly accused of exploitation in the developing countries, but economists have also noted a number of good effects they bring in their wake. Perhaps the chief good effect is what economists call spillover. This refers to the fact that domestic firms learn productivity-enhancing techniques from foreign corporations with better technology and management practices. Production workers often learn better techniques while employed by foreign firms. Managers may learn about better practices by observing, or by having previously worked at multinationals themselves. And increased competition pushes all companies in an area where multinationals are operating to become more productive.

In the movie *Manhattan*, Woody Allen's character talks about the hotel where the food is dreadful, and there was not enough of it, either! The critics of multinationals often make similar complaints. After arguing that multinationals must be condemned for exploiting workers and harming host countries wherever they go, critics sometimes inveigh against these same corporations for bypassing countries that need them, thereby widening the gap between the rich and the poor.

If multinationals avoid some poor countries, that is surely not surprising. They are businesses that must survive by making a profit—no corporation ever managed to do sustained good by continually posting losses. If a country wants to attract investment, it has to provide an attractive environment. That generally implies having political stability and economic advantages such as economical labor or useable natural resources. In the game of attracting investment, some countries are going to lose because they lack these attributes. The truly unfortunate countries are those experiencing acute problems of governance, as in the African countries ravaged by war.

It is unrealistic to expect multinationals to invest in these countries and "save" them, instead, the international community has to help them put their paralyzing conflicts and inadequate governance behind them over the long haul—a truly heroic task. In the meantime, the answer to such nations' pressing humanitarian and developmental needs must be public aid, technical assistance, and altruism from corporations and civil society groups. The World Bank ought to concentrate more on these problem states and should correspondingly turn away from lending to countries such as India and China, which now have the ability to develop by themselves. But, of course, the World Bank leadership seeks to maximize influence by distributing largesse to all; even altruistic institutions will occasionally be run by men whose private ambitions, rather than the social good, are the primary determinants of their policies.

# Globalization Has Helped Many Developing Countries

*John L. Manzella*

**About the author**: *John L. Manzella is a trade consultant and the author of the book,* Grasping Globalization: Its Impact and Your Corporate Response *(2005).*

The answer to the question, "has globalization harmed developing countries?," is "No!" Quite the contrary, in fact. Trade and globalization have improved the lives of billions of people in developing countries. For example, in the short span of 1990 through 1998, the number of people living in extreme poverty in East Asia and the Pacific decreased 41 percent—one of the largest and most rapid reductions in history.

## Openness to Trade Brings Development

Today, 24 developing countries representing about 3 billion people, including China, India and Mexico, have adopted policies enabling their citizens to take advantage of globalization. The net result is that their economies are catching up with rich ones.

Over the last two decades, according to the World Bank, these 24 countries achieved higher growth in incomes, longer life expectancy and better schooling. The incomes of the least globalized countries during this same period, including Iran, Pakistan and North Korea, dropped or remained static. What distinguishes the fastest growing developing countries from the slowest is clear: their openness to trade.

For many of the world's poorest countries, the primary problem is not too much globalization, but their inability to participate in it. Study after study corroborate this. For ex-

John L. Manzella, "Have Trade and Globalization Harmed Developing Countries?" *World Trade*, January 2006, vol. 19, iss. 1, p. 8.

ample, the WTO [World Trade Organization] report, *Trade, Income Disparity and Poverty*, says, "Trade liberalization helps poor countries catch up with rich ones," and concludes that trade liberalization "is essential if poor people are to have any hope of a brighter future."

*Globalization, Poverty and Inequality*, published by the Progressive Policy Institute, contends that less globalization is generally associated with less development, and concludes that no country has managed to lift itself out of poverty without integrating into the global economy.

And who would know this better than former Mexican President Ernesto Zedillo, who said, "In every case where a poor nation has significantly overcome its poverty, this has been achieved while engaging in production for export markets and opening itself to the influx of foreign goods, investment and technology—that is, by participating in globalization."

Even former sociologist Fernando Henrique Cardoso, who spoke out against aspects of global dependence, promoted—not resisted—globalization as president of Brazil.

Developing countries with open economies grew by 4.5 percent a year in the 1970s and 1980s, while those with closed economies grew by 0.7 percent a year, concludes the National Bureau of Economic Research report, Economic Convergence and Economic Policies. At this rate, open economies double in size every 16 years, while closed economies double every 100 years.

## More Globalization Needed

Globalization may not be a panacea for all economic ills, but it certainly helps alleviate them. However, it has had negative consequences on some developing countries with distorted economies or a lack of sound legal or financial systems. As a result, anti-globalists with good intentions but bad policy recommendations often make globalization the scapegoat for many of the world's problems.

In the end, the facts don't lie. Since the 1970s—when policies supporting globalization got traction—through 2001, world infant mortality rates decreased by almost half, adult literacy increased more than a third, primary school enrollment rose and the average life span shot up 11 years. Looking forward, from 2002 through 2025, life expectancy is projected to rise from 62 years to 68 years in less developed countries, the U.S. Census Bureau estimates.

The World Bank report, *Globalization, Growth and Poverty: Building an Inclusive World Economy*, suggests that globalization must be better harnessed to help the world's poorest, most marginalized countries improve the lives of their citizens—an especially important effort in the wake of September 11. Agreed. But how to achieve this is not yet known.

In the meantime consider this. If remaining world merchandise trade barriers are eliminated, potential gains are estimated at $250 to $650 billion annually, according to the International Monetary Fund and World Bank. About one-third to one-half of these gains would accrue in developing countries. Removal of agricultural supports would raise global economic welfare by an additional $128 billion annually, with some $30 billion going to developing countries.

# Globalization's Pain for Poor Countries Can Be Minimized

*Pranab Bardhan*

**About the author***: Pranab Bardhan, an economics professor at the University of California, Berkeley, was editor in chief of the* Journal of Development Economics *from 1985 to 2003, and is currently co-chair of a MacArthur Foundation–funded international research network on inequality and economic performance.*

Globalization and the attendant concerns about poverty and inequality have become a focus of discussion in a way that few other topics, except for international terrorism or global warming, have. Most people I know have a strong opinion on globalization, and all of them express an interest in the well-being of the world's poor. The financial press and influential international officials confidently assert that global free markets expand the horizons for the poor, whereas activist-protesters hold the opposite belief with equal intensity. Yet the strength of people's conviction is often in inverse proportion to the amount of robust factual evidence they have.

As is common in contentious public debates, different people mean different things by the same word. Some interpret "globalization" to mean the global reach of communications technology and capital movements, some think of the outsourcing by domestic companies in rich countries, and others see globalization as a byword for corporate capitalism or American cultural and economic hegemony. So it is best to be clear at the outset of this article that I shall primarily refer to economic globalization—the expansion of foreign trade and investment. How does this process affect the wages, in-

Pranab Bardhan, "Does Globalization Help or Hurt the World's Poor?" *Scientific American*, March 26, 2006, vol. 294, iss. 4, p. 84.

comes and access to resources for the poorest people in the world? This question is one of the most important in social science.

For a quarter century after World War II, most developing countries in Africa, Asia and Latin America insulated their economies from the rest of the world. Since then, though, most have opened their markets. For instance, between 1980 and 2000, trade in goods and services expanded from 23 to 46 percent of gross domestic product (GDP) in China and from 19 to 30 percent in India. Such changes have caused many hardships for the poor in developing countries but have also created opportunities that some nations utilize and others do not, largely depending on their *domestic* political and economic institutions. (The same is true for low-wage workers in the U.S., although the effects of globalization on rich countries are beyond the scope of this article.) The net outcome is often quite complex and almost always context-dependent, belying the glib pronouncements for or against globalization made in the opposing camps. Understanding the complexities is essential to taking effective action.

## Neither Plague nor Panacea

The case for free trade rests on the age-old principle of comparative advantage, the idea that countries are better off when they export the things they are best at producing, and import the rest. Most mainstream economists accept the principle, but even they have serious differences of opinion on the balance of potential benefits and actual costs from trade and on the importance of social protection for the poor. Free traders believe that the rising tide of international specialization and investment lifts all boats. Others point out that many poor people lack the capacity to adjust, retool and relocate with changing market conditions. These scholars argue that the benefits of specialization materialize in the long run, over which people and resources are assumed to be fully mobile, whereas the adjustments can cause pain in the short run. . . .

The debate among economists is a paragon of civility compared with the one taking place in the streets. Antiglobalizers' central claim is that globalization is making the rich richer and the poor poorer, proglobalizers assert that it actually helps the poor. But if one looks at the factual evidence, the matter is rather more complicated. On the basis of household survey data collected by different agencies, the World Bank estimates the fraction of the population in developing countries that falls below the $1-a-day poverty line (at 1993 prices)—an admittedly crude but internationally comparable level. By this measure, extreme poverty is declining in the aggregate.

---

*Integration into the international economy brings not only opportunities but also problems.*

---

The trend is particularly pronounced in East, South and Southeast Asia. Poverty has declined sharply in China, India and Indonesia—countries that have long been characterized by massive rural poverty and that together account for about half the total population of developing countries. Between 1981 and 2001 the percentage of rural people living on less than $1 a day decreased from 79 to 27 percent in China, 63 to 42 percent in India, and 55 to 11 percent in Indonesia. But although the poorest are not, on the whole, getting poorer, no one has yet convincingly demonstrated that improvements in their condition are mainly the result of globalization. In China the poverty trend could instead be attributed to internal factors such as the expansion of infrastructure, the massive 1978 land reforms (in which the Mao-era communes were disbanded), changes in grain procurement prices, and the relaxation of restrictions on rural-to-urban migration. In fact, a substantial part of the decline in poverty had already happened by the mid-1980s, before the big strides in foreign trade or investment. Of the more than 400 million Chinese lifted above the international poverty line between 1981 and 2001, three fourths got there by 1987.

In 2001 Naila Kabeer of the University of Sussex in England and Simeen Mahmud of the Bangladesh Institute of Development Studies did a survey of 1,322 women workers in Dhaka. They discovered that the average monthly income of workers in garment-export factories was 86 percent above that of the other wage workers living in the same slum neighborhoods.

Another indication of this relative improvement can be gauged by what happens when such opportunities disappear. In 1993, anticipating a U.S. ban on imports of products made using child labor, the garment industry in Bangladesh dismissed an estimated 50,000 children. UNICEF and local aid groups investigated what happened to them. About 10,000 children went back to school, but the rest ended up in much inferior occupations, including stone breaking and child prostitution. That does not excuse the appalling working conditions in the sweatshops, let alone the cases of forced or unsafe labor, but advocates must recognize the severely limited existing opportunities for the poor and the possible unintended consequences of "fair trade" policies.

## The Local Roots of Poverty

Integration into the international economy brings not only opportunities but also problems. Even when new jobs are better than the old ones, the transition can be wrenching. Most poor countries provide very little effective social protection to help people who have lost their jobs and not yet found new ones. Moreover, vast numbers of the poor work on their own small farms or for household enterprises. The major constraints they usually face are domestic, such as lack of access to credit, poor infrastructure, venal government officials and insecure land rights. Weak states, unaccountable regimes, lopsided wealth distribution, and inept or corrupt politicians and bureaucrats often combine to block out the opportunities for the poor. Opening markets without relieving these domestic constraints forces people to compete with one hand tied behind their back. The result can be deepened poverty.

Conversely, opening the economy to trade and long-term capital flows need not make the poor worse off if appropriate domestic policies and institutions are in place—particularly to help shift production to more marketable goods and help workers enter new jobs.

---

*There is no "race to the bottom" in which countries must abandon social programs to keep up economically.*

---

Contrasting case studies of countries make this quite apparent. Although the island economies of Mauritius and Jamaica had similar per capita incomes in the early 1980s, their economic performance since then has diverged dramatically, with the former having better participatory institutions and rule of law and the latter mired in crime and violence. South Korea and the Philippines had similar per capita incomes in the early 1960s, but the Philippines languished in terms of political and economic institutions (especially because power and wealth were concentrated in a few hands), so it remains a developing country, while South Korea has joined the ranks of the developed. Botswana and Angola are two diamond-exporting countries in southern Africa, the former democratic and fast-growing, the latter ravaged by civil war and plunder.

The experiences of these and other countries demonstrate that antipoverty programs need not be blocked by the forces of globalization. There is no "race to the bottom" in which countries must abandon social programs to keep up economically; in fact, social and economic goals can be mutually supportive. Land reform, expansion of credit and services for small producers, retraining and income support for displaced workers, public-works programs for the unemployed, and provision of basic education and health can enhance the productivity of workers and farmers and thereby contribute to a country's global competitiveness. Such programs may require a rethinking of budget priorities in those nations and a more accountable political and administrative framework, but the obstacles are largely domestic. Conversely, closing the economy to international trade does not reduce the power of the relevant vested interests: landlords, politicians and bureaucrats, and the rich who enjoy government subsidies. Thus, globalization is not the main cause of developing countries' problems, contrary to the claim of critics of globalization—just as globalization is often not the main solution to these problems, contrary to the claim of overenthusiastic free traders.

What about the environment? Many conservationists argue that international integration encourages the overexploitation of fragile natural resources, such as forests and fisheries, damaging the livelihoods of the poor. A common charge against transnational companies is that they flock to poor countries with lax environmental standards. Anecdotes abound, but researchers have done very few statistical studies. One of the few, published in 2003 by Gunnar Eskeland of the World Bank and Ann Harrison of the University of California, Berkeley, considered Mexico, Morocco, Venezuela and Ivory Coast. It found very little evidence that companies chose to invest in these countries to shirk pollution-abatement costs in rich countries; the single most important factor in determining the amount of investment was the size of the local market. Within a given industry, foreign plants tended to pollute less than their local peers.

Like persistent poverty, lax environmental standards are ultimately a domestic policy or institutional failure. A lack of well-defined or well-enforced property rights or regulation of common property resources often leads to their overuse. Responding to pressure from powerful political lobbies, governments have deliberately kept down the prices of precious environmental resources: irrigation water in India, energy in Russia, timber concessions in Indonesia and the Philippines. The result, unsurprisingly, is resource depletion. To be sure, if a country opens its markets without dealing with these distortions, it can worsen the environmental problems.

## When Talk Gives Way to Action

Fortunately, the two sides of the globalization debate are—slowly—developing some measure of agreement. In many areas, advocates in both camps see the potential for coordination among transnational companies, multilateral organizations, developing country governments and local aid groups on programs to help the poor. Going beyond the contentious debates and building on the areas of emerging consensus and cooperation, international partnerships may be able to make a dent in the poverty that continues to oppress the lives of billions of people in the world. Here are some measures under discussion.

Capital controls. The flow of international investment consists both of long-term capital (such as equipment) and of speculative short-term capital (such as shares, bonds and currency). The latter, shifted at the click of a mouse, can stampede around the globe in herdlike movements, causing massive damage to fragile economies. The Asian financial crisis of 1997 was an example. Following speculators' run on the Thai currency, the baht, the poverty rate in rural Thailand jumped 50 percent in just one year. In Indonesia, a mass withdrawal of short-term capital caused real wages in manufacturing to drop 44 percent. Many economists (including those who otherwise support free trade) now see a need for some form of control over short-term capital flows, particularly if domestic financial institutions and banking standards are weak. It is widely believed that China, India and Malaysia escaped the brunt of the Asian financial crisis because of their stringent controls on capital flight. Economists still disagree, though, on what form such control should take and what effect it has on the cost of capital.

Reduced protectionism. The major hurdle many poor countries face is not too much globalization but too little. It is hard for the poor of the world to climb out of poverty when rich countries (as well as the poor ones themselves) restrict imports and subsidize their own farmers and manufacturers. The annual loss to developing countries as a group from agricultural tariffs and subsidies in rich countries is estimated to be $45 billion; their annual loss from trade barriers on textile and clothing is estimated to be $24 billion. The toll exceeds rich countries' foreign aid to poor countries. Of course, the loss is not equally distributed among poor countries. Some would benefit more than others if these import restrictions and subsidies were lifted.

Trust-busting. Small exporters in poor nations often lack the marketing networks and brand names to make inroads into rich-country markets. Although transnational retail companies can help them, the margins and fees they charge are often very high. Restrictive business practices by these international middlemen are difficult to prove, but a great deal of circumstantial evidence exists. The international coffee market, for example, is dominated by four companies. In the early 1990s the coffee earnings of exporting countries were about $12 billion, and retail sales were $30 billion. By 2002 retail sales had more than doubled, yet coffee-producing countries received about half their earnings of a decade earlier. The problem is not global markets but impeded access to those markets or depressed prices received by producers, as a result of the near-monopoly power enjoyed by a few retail firms. In certain industries, companies may actively collude to fix prices. Some economists have proposed an international antitrust investigation agency. Even if such an agency did not have much enforcement power, it could mobilize public opinion and strengthen the hands of antitrust agencies in developing countries. In addition, internationally approved quality-certification programs can help poor-country products gain acceptance in global markets.

Social programs. Many economists argue that for trade to make a country better off, the government of that country may have to redistribute wealth and income to some extent, so that the winners from the policy of opening the economy share their gains with the losers. Of course, the phrase "to some extent" still leaves room for plenty of disagreement. Nevertheless, certain programs stir fairly little controversy, such as assistance programs to help workers cope with job losses and get retrained and redeployed. Scholarships allowing poor parents to send their children to school have proved to be more effective at reducing child labor than banning imports of products.

---

*Simplistic antiglobalization slogans or sermons on the unqualified benefits of free trade do not serve the cause of alleviating world poverty.*

---

Research. The Green Revolution played a major role in reducing poverty in Asia. New international private-public partnerships could help develop other products suitable for the poor (such as medicines, vaccines and crops). Under the current international patent regime, global pharmaceutical companies do not have much incentive to do costly research on diseases such as malaria and tuberculosis that kill millions of people in poor countries every year. But research collaborations are emerging among donor agencies, the World Health Organization, groups such as Doctors Without Borders and private foundations such as the Bill & Melinda Gates Foundation.

Immigration reform in rich countries. A program to permit larger numbers of unskilled workers into rich countries as "guest workers" would do more to reduce world poverty than other forms of international integration, such as trade liberalization, can. The current climate, however, is not very hospitable to this idea.

Simplistic antiglobalization slogans or sermons on the unqualified benefits of free trade do not serve the cause of alleviating world poverty. An appreciation of the complexity of the issues and an active interweaving of domestic and international policies would be decidedly more fruitful.

CHAPTER 3

# Will Globalization Destroy the Environment?

# Globalization and the Environment: An Overview

*Radley Balko*

**About the author**: *Radley Balko is a freelance writer living in Arlington, Virginia. Balko publishes his own blog,* The Agitator, *and writes occasionally for* Tech Central Station, *an online business and economics journal.*

What effects do trade agreements like NAFTA [North American Free Trade Agreement], GATT [General Agreement on Tariffs and Trade], and the WTO [World Trade Organization] have on the environment? What effects do they have on the environments of already developed countries versus the environmental integrity of the third world? If liberalized trade does indeed create wealth, does wealth and added industrialization better or worsen the developing world? Is there any way to have both—environmental protection *and* the benefits of free trade?

## The Free Trade Case: Opened vs. Closed Societies

In his book *Free Trade Under Fire*, [economist] Douglas Irwin writes:

> The greatest environmental disasters in recent years have taken place in Eastern Europe and the former Soviet Union. The horrible air pollution caused by state-run ... industries ... owe nothing to free trade, but resulted from a system of centralized decision-making that valued resources less wisely than a system of decentralized markets with well-established property rights and prudent government regulation.

Radley Balko, "Free Trade and the Environment," A World Connected, undated. www.aworldconnected.org/article.php/558.html.

Irwin of course is a free trader. And other free traders like him point out that in addition to being among the biggest polluters of the last century, the Soviet Union and Soviet Block countries were also among the most isolated countries of their era. With little trade or interaction with the outside world, with no markets to properly allocate resources, the Iron Curtain countries proved to be wasteful, dirty, and ultimately unaccountable in how they treated the environment, though the western world really only saw the extent of the damage after the Cold War.

*Only once the people in a given country are comfortable can they begin to demand the kinds of environmental standards the western world today takes for granted.*

At its 2001 meeting in Davos, Switzerland, the World Economic Forum [an international organization that engages buisness and other leaders in partnerships to solve world problems] released its "Sustainability Index," a ranking of the environmental health and environmental policy of 122 countries. At the top of the list were open, developed, primarily western countries, where high environmental standards accompany liberal trade policies and high standards of living, including the United States, Western Europe and Canada. The lowest-ranked countries tended to be those who have isolated themselves from the rest of the world with protectionist, inward-looking trade restrictions, including Saudi Arabia, Burundi, Ethiopia, and Libya. This, free traders say, isn't surprising. Free trade creates wealth. And only once the people in a given country are comfortable can they begin to demand the kinds of environmental standards the western world today takes for granted.

Even within the developing world, it is protectionist policies, not liberalization policies, that result in environmental damage. Irwin, for example, notes that there's a direct correlation between the amount of agricultural subsidies developing countries provide to their farmers and how much fertilizer those farmers use on their crops. The more subsidized the farm, the more likely it's using fertilizer. That's because subsidies are usually given to domestic industries to offset competitive advantages enjoyed by foreign competitors. If not for the subsidies, many farmers in Japan, for example, would likely find other work, leaving Japan's agriculture supply to foreign farmers better equipped for farming, and thus less likely to need fertilizers.

---

*Markets and private forces prove more adept at restraining pollution than government planning.*

---

Finally, even within a given country—developed or developing—markets and private forces prove more adept at restraining pollution than government planning. The World Bank notes that the worst individual polluters in the world are inevitably state-run enterprises, not private corporations. This, free traders say, is the most general defense against the accusation that the forces of globalization are hostile to the environment. Very generally, the evidence suggests that the more open and wealthy the society, the more market-oriented and competitive its economy is, the more likely it is to take care of its natural environment.

## The Anti-Globalization Case: The Race to the Bottom

On the anti-trade side, the familiar phrase "race to the bottom" is perhaps the most common criticism concerning how globalization threatens the environment. It's a phrase anti-globalists often use with respect to labor standards as well. The argument posits that if corporations are free to locate anywhere on the planet without the restraint of green regulations or restrictions, the world's poorest countries will re-lax—or simply eliminate—environmental standards in order to attract first world investment and the jobs and wealth that come with it.

On its website for student activists, for example, the Sierra Club writes that free trade pacts tie the hands of environmental regulators:

> Countries cannot make environmental or public health laws that may cause a company to lose profits, and if they do make such laws they have to pay the company back for every dollar of profit it loses (which can run to hundreds of millions of dollars). Countries cannot raise environmental or labor standards, because if they do, the corporations that have built factories in that country because of its cheap labor or lax enforcement of environmental laws will then threaten to move those factories to other places.

---

*As an economy switches from agriculture and subsistence living to crude manufacturing . . . that country can expect a temporary worsening of environmental conditions.*

---

In the 1994 book *Global Village or Global Pillage*, authors Jeremy Brecher and Tim Costello write:

> The race to the bottom is contributing to environmental destruction worldwide. Global corporations' oil refineries, steel mills, chemical plants, and other factories, now located all over the world, are the main source of greenhouse gases, ozone-depleting chemicals, and toxic pollutants. Their packaging is a major source of solid waste. . . .

> . . .The proportion of the Philippines that is forested has decreased from 35 percent to 20 percent—less than half the amount needed to maintain a stable ecosystem—just since 1969.

The argument is a compelling one. How can a developing country protect its environment and still attract needed investment if the country on its border is willing to relax its own environmental standards? . . .

## Short-Run Losses, Long-Run Gains?

Even the staunchest of free trade proponents will concede, however, that as free trade helps the most destitute of countries move from poverty to prosperity, we can expect to see at least some short-term negative impact on the environment. [The Cato Institute's Dan] Griswold writes, "Development itself can have a mixed impact on the environment. All else being equal, an economy that produces more of exactly the same goods and services in exactly the same way will produce more pollution." As an economy switches from agriculture and subsistence living to crude manufacturing, then, certainly that country can expect a temporary worsening of environmental conditions. Factories obviously produce more smoke than farms. Old cars and scooters emit more fumes than camels, horses, or donkeys.

By most indications, however, this pollution-intensive phase is short-lived. As industrialization creates wealth, wealth enables new industries to employ more modern, more environmentally friendly technology. And as citizens rise from poverty to the middle class, they tend to become less concerned about their own survival, and more concerned about their surroundings. The economists Gene Grossman and Alan Krueger write in a 1994 paper for the National Bureau of Economic Research, "We find no evidence that environmental quality deteriorates steadily with economic growth. Rather, for most indicators, economic growth brings an initial phase of deterioration followed by a subsequent phase of improvement."

Griswold and other economists call this phenomenon the "green ceiling." Once a country's income level reaches a certain level, its citizens begin to demand better environmental standards, and its corporations and its government can afford to implement them. Grossman and Krueger put the "green ceiling" at about $5,000 per capita GDP. But there's evidence that with today's technology, interconnectivity and world economy, even that number may be falling. A recent World Bank study on water pollution, for example concluded that "pollution intensity falls by 90 per cent as per capita income rises from $500 to $20,000, with the fastest decline occurring *before* the country reaches middle income status." A World Bank briefing paper on globalization states, "... it is striking that many developing countries have already turned or are turning the corner in the fight against pollution at much lower levels of income than the rich countries did in their day."

---

*Free traders argue that some short-term environmental damage may be necessary as ... countries struggle to build the requisite wealth to make way for cleaner surroundings.*

---

Free traders point to lots of anecdotal evidence to support the "green ceiling" theory. Since China began liberalizing its trade policy in the 1980s, for example, air quality in its major cities has either stabilized or improved. Griswold notes that since the passage of NAFTA, a more affluent Mexico City has been able to introduce cleaner gasoline, and residents there have begun installing catalytic converters on their automobiles. As a result, Mexico City's air quality has dramatically improved over the last ten years, and is cleaner today than the air in Los Angeles was 30 years ago.

## So Who's Right?

There's no question that the world's most affluent countries also happen to be its cleanest (though environmentalists would counter that richer countries also consume more resources).

And there's no question that agrarian, subsistence economies are more environmentally friendly than economies in the first stages of industrialization.

The debate seems to be over how to bring the world's poorest countries from the depths of poverty to affluence and comfort with minimal damage to the environment.

Free traders argue that some short-term environmental damage may be necessary as those countries struggle to build the requisite wealth needed to make way for cleaner surroundings. Opponents argue that international standards and regulations are needed from the start to ensure that western corporations don't spoil untouched habitats for profit.

It's clear that international trade is only likely to expand, and that environmental awareness too has taken hold of the international community. As free trade zones multiply, and as advocacy organizations push border-crossing regulatory agendas, it's also clear that while there is still a debate, we'll soon have more opportunity to see the results effected by both approaches.

# The Pressures of Globalization Will Produce Unprecedented Environmental Deterioration

*James Gustave Speth*

**About the author**: *James Gustave Speth is dean and professor at the School of Forestry & Environmental Studies at Yale University. He founded and was president of the World Resources Institute and served as advisor on environmental issues for Presidents Carter and Clinton.*

We live in the twenty-first century, but we live with the twentieth century. The expansion of the human enterprise in the twentieth century, and especially after World War II, was phenomenal. It was in this century that human society truly left the moorings of its past and launched itself upon the planet in an unprecedented way.

Most familiar is the population explosion. It took all of human history for global population to expand by 1900 to a billion and a half people. But over the past century that many more people were added, on average, every thirty-three years. In the past twenty-five years, global population increased by 50 percent from four to six billion, with virtually all of this growth occurring in the developing world.

Population may have increased fourfold in the past century, but world economic output increased twentyfold. From the dawn of history to 1950 the world economy grew to seven trillion dollars. It now grows by this amount every five to ten years. Since 1960 the size of the world economy has doubled and then doubled again. Energy use moved in close step with economic expansion, rising at least sixteenfold in the twenti-

James Gustave Speth, *Red Sky at Morning: America and the Crisis of the Global Environment*. New Haven, CT: Yale University Press, 2004, pp. 11–22.

eth century. One calculation suggests that more energy was consumed in those hundred years than in all of previous history.

## The Environmental Impact of the Twentieth Century

The twentieth century was thus a remarkable period of prodigious expansion in human populations and their production and consumption. . . . While twentieth-century growth has brought enormous benefits in terms of health, education, and overall standards of living, these gains have been purchased at a huge cost to the environment. The enormous environmental deterioration is partly due to the greater scale of established insults: traditional pollution like soot, sulfur oxides, and sewage grew from modest quantities to huge ones. What were once strictly local impacts not only intensified locally but became regional and even global in scope.

---

*Twentieth-century expansion . . . pushed the human enterprise and its effects to planetary scale.*

---

Many previously unknown environmental risks also surfaced in the twentieth century. After World War II, the chemical and nuclear industries emerged, giving rise to a vast armada of new chemicals and radioactive substances, many highly biocidal in even the most minute quantities and some with the potential to accumulate in biological systems or in the atmosphere. Between 1950 and 1985 the U.S. chemical industry expanded its output tenfold. By 1985 the number of hazardous waste sites in the United States requiring clean-up was estimated to be between two thousand and ten thousand. The use of pesticides also skyrocketed during this period. Today about six hundred pesticides are registered for use around the world, and five to six billion pounds of pesticides are released into the global environment each year.

Turning from pollution to the world's natural resource base we find severe losses. From a third to a half of the world's forests are now gone, as are about half the mangroves and other wetlands. Agricultural productivity of a fourth of all usable land has been significantly degraded due to overuse and mismanagement. In 1960, 5 percent of marine fisheries were either fished to capacity or overfished; today 75 percent of marine fisheries are in this condition. A crisis in the loss of bio-diversity is fast upon us. A fourth of bird species are extinct, and another 12 percent are listed as threatened. Also threatened are 24 percent of mammals, 25 percent of reptiles, and 30 percent of fish species. The rate of species extinction today is estimated to be a hundred to a thousand times the normal rate at which species disappear. . . .

The twentieth-century expansion is significant because it has pushed the human enterprise and its effects to planetary scale. This is the globalization of environmental impacts as well as economic activity. Human influences in the environment are everywhere, affecting all natural systems and cycles. Environmental writer Bill McKibben wrote in 1989 about what he called "the end of nature," by which he meant the end of the millennia in which humanity could view nature as a force independent of human beings. Previously it was possible to think of nature as a place free of human control, an external and complex system sustaining life on earth, but the twentieth century brought us across a threshold to a new reality. . . .

## The Future of Globalized Economic Development

Economic growth will continue to expand dramatically in this century. With population poised to grow by 25 percent over the next twenty years, with people everywhere striving to better themselves, and with governments willing to go to extraordinary measures to sustain high levels of economic expansion, there is no reason to think that the world economy will not double and perhaps double again within the lifetimes of today's young people.

The next doubling of world economic activity will surely differ in some respects from the growth of the past. But there are good reasons to believe that that doubling could, from an environmental perspective, look a lot like the last. The pressures to persist with environmentally problematic technologies and practices are enormous. The U.S. Energy Information Agency projects that global emissions of carbon dioxide, the principal climate-altering gas, will increase by 60 percent between 2001 and 2025. The Paris-based Organization for Economic Cooperation and Development estimates that its members' carbon dioxide emissions will go up by roughly a third between 1995 and 2020 if there is not major policy intervention, while OECD motor vehicle use could rise by almost 40 percent. During this same period, emissions of carbon dioxide outside the OECD are projected to go up 100 percent. Growing food demand is expected to increase the area under cultivation in Africa and Latin America, extending agriculture further into once-forested areas and onto fragile lands in semiarid zones. For this reason and others, countries outside the OECD are projected to lose another 15 percent of their forests by 2020.

One area where growing populations and growing demands will come together to challenge us enormously is water—the supply of clean, fresh water. The United Nations' 2003 *World Water Development Report* concludes that twenty-five years of international conferences have yielded few solutions. A fifth of the world's people lack clean drinking water; 40 percent lack sanitary services. Between 1970 and 1990 water supplies per person decreased by a third globally and are likely to drop by a further third over the next twenty years absent a concerted international response. Peter Aldhous, the chief news editor at *Nature*, puts the situation with water in perspective: "The water crisis is real. If action isn't taken, millions of people will be condemned to a premature death. . . . [P]opulation growth, pollution and climate change are conspiring to exacerbate the situation. Over the next two decades, the average supply of water per person will drop by a third. Heightened hunger and disease will follow. Humanity's demands for water also threaten natural ecosystems, and may bring nations into conflicts that—although they may not lead to war—will test diplomats' skills to the limit." The U.N. report notes that to meet internationally agreed water supply and sanitation targets, 342,000 additional people will have to be provided with sanitation every day until 2015.

---

*We have entered the endgame in our traditional, historical relationship with the natural world.*

---

Of course, economic growth can generate benefits for the environment, and has done so in many contexts. As people become wealthier, public support for a healthy environment and leisure activities based on nature increases. The press of the poor on the resource base can diminish as people live less close to the land. Governments of well-to-do countries tend to be more capable regulators and managers and can have more revenue for environmental, family planning, and other programs. There is no doubt that some important environmental indicators, such as sanitation, improve with rising incomes. But it is extraordinarily misguided to conclude from such considerations, as some do, that the world can simply grow out of its environmental problems. Were that true, the rich countries would have long ago solved their environmental challenges, and we would not have projections such as those just cited from the OECD and the United Nations. In developing countries undergoing rapid industrialization, new environmental problems (such as truly terrible urban air pollution and acid rain and smog over large regions) are replacing old ones. Collectively the environmental impacts of rich and poor have mounted as the world economy has grown, and we have not yet deployed the means to reduce the human footprint on the planet faster than the economy expands. . . .

## An Environmental Endgame

The implications of all this are profound. We have entered the endgame in our traditional, historical relationship with the natural world. The current Nature Conservancy campaign has an appropriate name: they are seeking to protect the Last Great Places. We are in a race to the finish. Soon, metaphorically speaking, whatever is not protected will be paved. . . . Whatever slack nature once cut us is gone.

Humans dominate the planet today as never before. We now live in a full world. An unprecedented responsibility for planetary management is now thrust upon us, whether we like it or not. This huge new burden, for which there is no precedent and little preparation, is the price of our economic success. We brought it upon ourselves, and we must turn to it with urgency and with even greater determination and political attention than has been brought to liberalizing trade and making the world safe for market capitalism. The risks of inaction extend beyond unprecedented environmental deterioration. Following closely in its wake would be widespread loss of livelihoods, social tensions and conflict, and huge economic costs.

# Environmental Damage Is Intrinsic to the Globalization Process

*Jerry Mander*

**About the author**: *Jerry Mander is the founder and president of the International Foundation on Globalization, an alliance of sixty organizations in twenty five countries formed to stimulate new thinking, joint activity, and public education in response to economic globalization.*

Among many preposterous claims, advocates of economic globalization argue that it increases long-term environmental protection. The theory goes that as countries globalize, often by exploiting resources like forests, minerals, oil, coal, fish, wildlife, and water, their increased wealth will enable them to save more patches of nature from their ravages and they will be able to introduce technical devices to mitigate the negative environmental impacts of their own increased production. There is ample evidence, however, that when countries increase their apparent receipts in a global economy, most of the benefit goes to global corporations who have little incentive to put their profits back into environmental protection. Instead, they plow them back into further exploitation, or they just take the money and run, right out of the country. This is normal corporate behavior in a global economy....

In fact, economic globalization itself—the very ideologies and structures that drive it—is intrinsically opposed to the survival of nature. No environmental side agreements or pollution controls or techno-fixes can mitigate the inherent environmental harms of a globalized economy with its export-oriented production models; the problems are built into the

Jerry Mander, "Economic Globalization and the Environment," *Tikkun*, September 2001, vol. 16, iss. 5, p. 33.

design. If we are going to proceed with this global experiment, we are going to have some predictable outcomes, and they are unavoidable. They are intrinsic to the form. . . .

## Globalization a Human Creation

Advocates of globalization love to describe it as a done deal, the result of economic and technological forces that have simply evolved over centuries to their present form. They describe it as if it was an uncontrollable, undirected force of nature. Of course, if we accepted this description of the inevitability of globalization, as most media, governments, and universities tend to do, then obviously no resistance would be possible. . . .

Of course it's true enough that global trade activity and concepts like "free trade" have indeed existed for centuries in various forms. But earlier versions were entirely different from the modern version in scale, speed, form, impact, and, most importantly, intent. The modern version of economic globalization definitely did not simply evolve, as in nature, like some kind of naturally dominant plant or animal species, an economic kudzu vine. Modern globalization is no accident of evolution. It was created by human beings, on purpose, and with a specific goal: to give primacy to corporate values above all other values, and to aggressively install and codify those values globally.

In fact, the modern globalization era has a birth date and birthplace: the fateful meetings at Bretton Woods, New Hampshire, in July 1944. That was when the world's leading corporate figures, economists, politicians, and bankers got together to figure out how to mitigate the devastation of World War II. They decided that a new centralized global economic system was required to promote global economic development. This would lead away from wars, they thought, and would help the poor and the rebuilding process.

Out of the Bretton Woods meetings came the World Bank, the International Monetary Fund [IMF] . . . and then the

General Agreement on Tariffs and Trade [GATT], which later gave birth to the World Trade Organization [WTO]. Later clones of the model included NAFTA [North American Free Trade Agreement], the Maastricht Agreement in Europe, the upcoming Free Trade Area of the Americas Agreement [FTAA], and quite a few others.

Together these instruments of economic globalization have been fulfilling their mandate, which is arguably to bring the most fundamental redesign of the planet's social, economic, and political arrangements at least since the Industrial Revolution. They are engineering a power shift of stunning proportions, moving real economic and political power away from national, state, and local governments and communities toward a new centralized model that gives great power to global corporations, banks, and the global bureaucracies they helped create, albeit with grave consequences for national sovereignty, community control, democracy, indigenous cultures, and more to the point today, the natural world.

The crucial point to remind ourselves about is that this process—these institutions and the rules they operate by—have been created on purpose by human beings and corporations and economists and bankers, and have specific forms designed for specific outcomes. It is no accident. It was not inevitable. And it can be reversed or revised, if with difficulty. What, then, can we say about the form?

## Economic Growth Valued Above Environmental Laws

The first tenet of economic globalization, as now designed, is to integrate and merge all economic activity of all countries on the planet within a single, homogenized model of development; a single centralized super system. . . . A second tenet of the globalization design is that primary importance is given to the achievement of ever more rapid, and never ending economic growth—let's call it "hypergrowth"—fueled by the con-

stant search for access to new resources, new and cheaper labor sources, and new markets. . . . So it's the job of the Bretton
Woods instruments to assist this commodification, privatization, deregulation, and free trade by creating rules that require
nations not only to conform to these principles, but also to
actively try to eliminate impediments within individual nations that might restrict corporate access to markets, labor,
and resources. In practice, most of these so-called impediments to the system are laws that are legally created by governments: environmental laws, public health laws, food safety
laws, laws that pertain to protecting worker rights and opportunities, laws that allow nations to control who can invest on
their soil, who can buy their currencies, and at what speed
and under what conditions. . . . All of these laws, even if created by democratic governments through democratic processes acting on behalf of the popular views of citizens, are
viewed by free traders as "non-tariff barriers to trade" and as
obstacles subject to WTO challenges.

---

*They love to call it "free trade," but what they really
mean by "free trade" is freedom for global corporations.*

---

Though it is only six [today, eleven] years old, the WTO
already has an impressive record of challenging democratically
created laws and standards. It's been particularly potent in the
environmental realm. The WTO's very first ruling was against
the U.S. Clean Air Act, which set high standards against polluting gasoline. The Act was found to be noncompliant with
WTO trade rules and had to be softened. The very popular
Marine Mammal Protection Act—particularly the provision
that protects dolphins otherwise killed by industrial tuna fishing—was found noncompliant under a GATT rule, now within
the WTO. And sea turtle protections under the Endangered
Species Act were also found illegal. The United States is going
back to the drawing board on these. We can expect similar

challenges against U.S. or state pesticide control laws, CAFE [Corporate Average Fuel Economy] standards, raw log export bans, ecolabeling of products, various "certification" schemes, et al.

The WTO doesn't rule only against U.S. environmental laws. It also ruled against Japan for refusing imports of fruit products carrying dangerous invasive species. It ruled against the European Union for forbidding imports of U.S. beef injected with biotech growth hormone, even though the European public is totally against biotech. In agriculture areas, the WTO has consistently ruled in favor of large machine- and chemical-intensive global industrial ag corporations over small-scale family farming and indigenous farmers—most appallingly in the famous Chiquita banana case. That case held that the European Union could not favor small indigenous, often organic farmers within former European colonies over the industrial bananas from Chiquita. . . .

---

*Every mile of . . . increased transport activity in the global economy has tremendous costs to the environment.*

---

There are hundreds of similar cases and examples. These trade bodies exist for the purpose of providing global corporations an easy way to circumvent the laws that attempt to regulate them. They love to call it "free trade," but what they really mean by "free trade" is freedom for global corporations; these same rules in fact suppress the freedoms for communities or nations to regulate or otherwise maintain their primary values, from environmental sustainability to local approaches to health, culture, jobs, and national sovereignty—even to democracy itself. . . .

## The Environmental Effects of Export-Oriented Production

Arguably the most important principle of free trade is its emphasis on global conversion to export-oriented production as some kind of economic and social nirvana. This is the theory that all countries should specialize their production within commodity areas where they have a so-called "comparative advantage" over other countries. Their advantage could be in coffee production or sugarcane or forest products or high tech due to unusually low wages. Each country should focus on these few specialized areas and then try to satisfy its other needs through imports, using foreign exchange earned by exports to pay for imports. This is a crucial component of globalization theory: the idea that it is necessary to replace diverse local or regional economic systems, systems that may emphasize highly diversified, small scale, industrial, artisanal, and agriculture systems, featuring many small producers using mostly local or regional resources and local labor, and consumed locally or regionally. The goal is to replace these diverse systems with large monocultural export systems. . . .

The central feature of an export-oriented model is obviously that it increases transport and shipping activity. In the half century since Bretton Woods, there has been about a twenty-five-fold increase in global transport activity. My friend and colleague, Minneapolis economist David Morris, loves to use the example of a toothpick, which comes wrapped in plastic and is marked, "Made in Japan." Japan is skilled in industrial production—that's one of its "comparative advantages"—but it has very few trees and no oil. But in a global economy, it is somehow thought efficient to ship wood from some country that grows it—Chile, Canada, the United States—and also to ship some barrels of oil to Japan, then wrap the one in the other, package them in serviceable commodity units, and ship them back across oceans to consumers. That toothpick, by the time it is finally used, might have traveled 50,000 miles. . . .

Every mile of such increased transport activity in the global economy has tremendous costs to the environment, costs which remain externalized by our current measures of efficiency, that is, costs which eventually are subsidized by taxpayers. For example, as global transport increases, it requires a massive increase in global infrastructure development. This is good for large corporations like Bechtel, who get to do the construction work, but it's bad news for the environments where such infrastructures are needed: new airports, new seaports, new oilfields, new pipelines for the oil, new rail lines, new high speed highways. . . .

Even more important is the increase in fossil fuel use. Ocean shipping carries nearly 80 percent of the world's international trade in goods. The fuel that's commonly used is a mixture of diesel and low quality oil known as "Bunker C" which is particularly polluting and very high in carbon and sulfur. If not consumed by ships, it would otherwise be considered a waste product. The shipping industry is anticipating major growth over the next few years; the port of Los Angeles alone projects a 50 percent increase over the next decade.

Increased air transport is even worse than shipping. Each ton of freight moved by plane uses forty-nine times as much energy per kilometer than when it's moved by ship. One physicist at Boeing likened the pollution from the takeoff of a single 747 to "setting the local gas station on fire and flying it over your neighborhood." A two-minute takeoff of a 747 is equal to 2.4 million lawnmowers running for twenty minutes. It is now estimated by many that the increase of global transport is one of the largest contributors to the growing crisis of climate change. . . .

## Effects on People

In the end, the most traumatic social and environmental consequences of economic globalization occur at the regional and local levels, especially because of the shift from economies based on small-scale, diverse models of agricultural production, to the industrial export model. The results are grim.

We must remember that nearly half of the world population still lives directly on the land, growing food for their families and communities. They emphasize staples and other mixed crops and they replant with indigenous seed varieties, using crop rotation and community sharing of resources like water, seeds, labor, and so forth. Such systems have kept them going for a millennia. But, as I said earlier, local systems are anathema to global corporations. So companies like Monsanto, Cargill, and Archer Daniels Midland are leading a chorus of corporate, government, and bureaucratic statements— often expressed in millions of dollars worth of ads—that small farmers are not "productive" or "efficient" enough to feed a hungry world. Only global corporations can do it. . . .

As for the people who used to live on the lands, growing their own foods, they are rapidly being removed from their lands. And they are not getting jobs, either. Since these corporate systems feature highly intensive, machine- and pesticide-driven production, there are very few jobs. So the people who used to feed themselves become landless, cashless, homeless, dependent, and hungry! Communities that were once self-sustaining disappear, and still intact cultures are decimated. This is so even in this country, where there are now very few family farmers left.

Eventually, the farmers and their families flee to crowded urban slums. There, without community, without cultural supports, they try to compete for the rare poorly paid urban job. Families that once fed themselves become society's burden, while huge corporate farmers get rich from exports. . . .

## Who Benefits?

One could grant the benefit of the doubt to the architects of this global experiment. Let's say they meant well. Maybe they really believed that this system would produce a kind of rapid exponential growth that would be truly beneficial. We have certainly heard them repeat the main homily over and over: "A rising tide will lift all boats." This is the claim that globalization's benefits will trickle down to all segments of society; that, indeed, its real purpose is to help lift the poor. But is that true?

First of all, how can hyperexpansion be sustained? How long can it go on before we have to directly face the limits of a finite planet? Where will the resources—the minerals, the wood, the water, the power—come from to feed an exponential expansion, without killing the planet? How many cars and refrigerators can be built and bought? How many roads can cover the landscape? How many fish can be industrially vacuumed from the sea before the ecosystem fails, and the species disappear? How much pollution can we live with? or global warming? or ozone depletion before the social and environmental costs become too great?

---

*Of the largest economies in the world, 52 are now corporations.*

---

And who, finally, benefits? It's not the farmers driven from their lands and made into homeless refugees. It's not urban dwellers, dealing with influxes of displaced peoples, jamming in to look for jobs. It's not workers caught in downward wage spirals. It's surely not nature.

Well. . . . Here in the United States we know that top corporate executives of the largest global companies are making salaries and options in the millions of dollars, often in the hundreds of millions, while real wages of ordinary workers have been declining. . . . The U.N. Development Program 1999 report indicated that the gap between the wealthy and the poor within and among countries of the world is getting steadily larger, and it blamed inherent inequities in the global trade system. And such is the degree of wealth concentration from all this, that the world's 475 billionaires are now worth the combined incomes of the bottom 50 percent of humanity.

Of the largest 100 economies in the world, 52 are now corporations. Mitsubishi is the twenty-second largest economy in the world. GM is twenty-sixth. Ford is thirty-first. All are larger than Denmark, Thailand, Turkey, South Africa, Saudi Arabia, Norway, Finland, Malaysia, Chile, New Zealand.

And if you still cling to the nostalgic idea that big corporations are helping employ the global workforces—that size begets jobs—here's one final stat: the 200 largest corporations in the world now account for about 30 percent of global economic activity, but employ less than half of one percent of the global work force. As these companies continue to get larger and more globalized, they continue to replace workers with machines, or buy up competitors and eliminate duplicate jobs. Such economies of scale are intrinsic to the free trade globalization design, just as environmental pollution is intrinsic to export-oriented trade. Large scale mergers and consolidations produces fewer jobs, not more jobs.

So much for the rising tide that lifts all boats. Clearly it lifts only yachts.

# In Mexico, Free Trade Has Led to Large-Scale Environmental Degradation

*Kevin P. Gallagher*

**About the author**: *Kevin P. Gallagher is a research associate at the Global Development and Environment Institute at the Fletcher School of Law and Diplomacy at Tufts University. He is also the author of the book,* Free Trade and the Environment: Mexico, NAFTA, and Beyond *(2004).*

During the NAFTA [North American Free Trade Agreement] negotiations, proponents of the agreement argued that free trade would lead to seemingly automatic improvements in environmental conditions in countries like Mexico. Opponents of NAFTA said that the environment would automatically worsen in Mexico because Mexico's lower standards would attract highly polluting firms from the United States. In effect, Mexico would serve as a pollution haven for U.S. industry. Ten years after NAFTA, what happened?

## The Free Traders' Argument

The [NAFTA] proponents were generalizing from the so-called "environmental Kuznets curve" (EKC) hypothesis. The name derives from an analogy to the original Kuznets curve—the theory that inequality first increases, then later decreases, as per capita income grows over time. Studies in the early 1990s reported a similar relationship between environmental degradation and levels of income: environmental degradation may sharply increase in the early stages of economic development, but the rise in per capita income past a certain "turning point" seemed to gradually reduce environmental damage.

Kevin P. Gallagher, "Mexico, NAFTA, and Beyond," *Americas Program of the Interhemispheric Resource Center*, September 17, 2004. http://ase.tufts.edu/gdae/Pubs/rp/NAFTAEnviroKGAmerProgSep04.pdf.

Economists hypothesized that environmental improvement beyond the "turning point" happened for three reasons. First are so-called scale effects: increases in growth correspond with increases in pollution. However, scale effects can be offset by what are called composition and technique effects. Composition effects occur when economies shift shifts toward services and other less pollution-intensive economic activities. Finally, technique effects occur when increasing income eventually leads to higher levels of environmental awareness, which translates into more stringent environmental policies as the growing middle class demands a cleaner environment.

---

*[In Mexico,] rises in income have been small and environmental degradation has been large.*

---

Early EKC studies suggested the "turning point" at which economies would begin to get less pollution-intensive was a per capita income of approximately $5,000. This led to the policy prescription now heard in many negotiating rooms: that the environment can wait, since economic growth will eventually (and naturally) result in environmental improvement. More recent studies, however, have called into question both the specific findings and the broad generalizations from these early EKC studies.

## Environmental Degradation in Mexico

Mexico reached $5,000 GDP per capita in 1985 (in PPP terms), precisely the year it began opening its economy. The data suggest, however, that subsequent rises in income have been small and environmental degradation has been large. Statistics from Mexico's National Institute for Statistics, Geography, and Information Systems (INEGI) document how environmental degradation has overwhelmed any benefits from trade-led economic growth.

First, since 1985 real incomes have grown at just 2.5% per year, and less than one percent per capita. Second, according to INEGI, major environmental problems have worsened since trade liberalization began in Mexico. Despite the fact that Mexico reached levels of income beyond the range of a predicted EKC turning point, national levels of soil erosion, municipal solid waste, and urban air and water pollution all worsened from 1985 to 1999. Rural soil erosion grew by 89%, municipal solid waste by 108%, water pollution by 29%, and urban air pollution by 97%.

The results have been costly to Mexico's prospects for development. The INEGI studies estimate the financial costs of this environmental degradation at 10% of GDP [gross domestic product] from 1988 to 1999, an average of $36 billion of damage each year ($47 billion for 1999). The destruction overwhelms the value of economic growth, which has been just 2.5% annually, or $14 billion per year.

## Is Mexico a Pollution Haven?

Is the Mexican environment worsening because Mexico is serving as a pollution haven for highly polluting industries in the United States? A number of studies analyze the extent to which economic activity in pollution-intensive industries expanded in Mexico before and after NAFTA. One would expect that the amount of pollution-intensive industry would decrease in the United States and increase in Mexico. What was found, however, was that the amount of dirty industry decreased more in Mexico than in the United States.

The reason why there is little evidence for pollution havens in developing countries is that the economic costs of environmental regulation and compliance are relatively small compared to other factors of production—especially those that determine comparative advantage. Mexico has an abundance of unskilled labor that finds employment primarily in manufacturing assembly plants. On average, such production processes are less pollution-intensive than more capital-laden manufacturing activities such as cement, pulp and paper, and base metals production. Economic activity in the latter sectors has actually fallen off in Mexico during the NAFTA period. Even at the margin, the costs of pollution control are too small to significantly factor into the average firm's location decisions. In addition, many firms are simply too large and cumbersome to move to another location, and they need to stay close to their product markets. The marginal abatement costs are small relative to the transaction costs of decommissioning and actually moving to another country.

---

*[Environmental] degradation is occurring because the proper mechanisms were not put in place to help Mexico manage its economic growth in an environmentally sustainable manner.*

---

Although the majority of firms that move to Mexico do not move there because of low environmental standards, this does not imply that when firms move to Mexico they are model environmental corporations. In fact, the World Bank conducted a survey of over 200 firms in Mexico and found that, contrary to prevailing assumptions, foreign firms were no more likely than domestic firms to comply with Mexican environmental law.

## Need for Strong Environmental Institutions

If the Mexican environment is worsening, but not because it is a pollution haven, what is driving environmental degradation? Costly degradation is occurring because the proper mechanisms were not put in place to help Mexico manage its economic growth in an environmentally sustainable manner. In the lead-up to NAFTA, Mexico doubled spending on environmental protection and started a much-needed industrial environmental inspection program. However, shortly after

NAFTA was signed and fiscal and financial woes set in, attention to the environment nose-dived. According to INEGI, since 1994 real spending on environmental protection declined by the equivalent of $200 million, or 45%. Even at their highest levels, allocations for environmental protection were low in comparison to Mexico's counterparts in the OECD [Organisation for Economic Cooperation and Development]; as a percentage of GDP, they were only one-fifth that of other OECD nations. Tellingly, the number of industrial environmental inspections has also decreased by 45% over the same period.

The environmental "side" institutions created by NAFTA set some important precedents, but were not equipped to address these problems. At most, Mexico receives only one-third of the $9 million annual budget of the North American Commission for Environmental Cooperation (NACEC). NACEC has been effective in carrying out its limited mandate, enabling citizen groups to monitor environmental progress and convening cross-national information sharing and research efforts in North America. But its $3 million budget is dwarfed by Mexico's budget shortfalls and buried by the $36 billion price tag of environmental degradation.

## Environmental Lessons From NAFTA

There is no evidence that pollution has begun to decrease now that Mexico has passed the theoretical turning point of $5,000 per capita. Nor have other environmental indicators begun to show improvement. This study also suggests that fears that NAFTA would create a pollution haven for dirty industry in Mexico were not justified overall, though the firms that have moved to Mexico have not always followed environmental best practice.

Together, these findings suggest two important conclusions as countries continue to negotiate the terms under which they will integrate into the global economy. First, if growth alone will not bring with it a long-term tendency toward environmental improvement, or if the turning point is so distant as to make the environmental costs of waiting unacceptable, then governments need to put in place the institutional mechanisms that can monitor environmental impacts and prevent unacceptable levels of environmental destruction. Without environmental laws, regulations, and the willingness and capacity to enforce them, trade-led growth will lead to increases in environmental degradation.

Second, since the evidence from Mexico suggests that environmental regulations and enforcement are not generally decisive in most firms' location decisions, governments should have little fear in strengthening such safeguards. Governments will not be jeopardizing their access to foreign direct investment by enacting strong environmental legislation and enforcing it.

In short, governments need to act to protect their environments. The costs of doing so, in terms of lost investment, are likely to be very low. The costs of inaction are likely to be very high.

# Current Global Business Practices Harm the Environment

*Al Gore and David Blood*

**About the authors**: *Al Gore is a former vice president of the United States and is currently chairman of Generation Investment Management, an employee-owned investment company that focuses on sustainable business practices. David Blood is a former head of Goldman Sachs Asset Management and today is managing partner of Generation Investment Management, which he co-founded with Mr. Gore.*

Capitalism and sustainability are deeply and increasingly interrelated. After all, our economic activity is based on the use of natural and human resources. Not until we more broadly "price in" the external costs of investment decisions across all sectors will we have a sustainable economy and society.

## Current Unsustainable Business Practices

The industrial revolution brought enormous prosperity, but it also introduced unsustainable business practices. Our current system for accounting was principally established in the 1930s by Lord [John Maynard] Keynes and the creation of "national accounts" (the backbone of today's gross domestic product). While this system was precise in its ability to account for capital goods, it was imprecise in its ability to account for natural and human resources because it assumed them to be limitless. This, in part, explains why our current model of economic development is hard-wired to externalize as many costs as possible.

Al Gore and David Blood, "For People and Planet," *The Wall Street Journal*, April 3, 2006.

Externalities are costs created by industry but paid for by society. For example, pollution is an externality which is sometimes taxed by government in order to make the entity responsible "internalize" the full costs of production. Over the past century, companies have been rewarded financially for maximizing externalities in order to minimize costs.

## Sustainability Is the Way Forward

Today, the global context for business is clearly changing. "Capitalism is at a crossroads," says Stuart Hart, professor of management at Cornell University. We agree, and we think the financial markets have a significant opportunity to chart the way forward. In fact, we believe that sustainable development will be the primary driver of industrial and economic change over the next 50 years.

The interests of shareholders, over time, will be best served by companies that maximize their financial performance by strategically managing their economic, social, environmental and ethical performance. This is increasingly true as we confront the limits of our ecological system to hold up under current patterns of use. "License to operate" can no longer be taken for granted by business as challenges such as climate change, HIV/AIDS, water scarcity and poverty have reached a point where civil society is demanding a response from business and government. The "polluter pays" principle is just one example of how companies can be held accountable for the full costs of doing business. Now, more than ever, factors beyond the scope of Keynes's national accounts are directly affecting a company's ability to generate revenues, manage risks, and sustain competitive advantage. There are many examples of the growing acceptance of this view.

## Companies with Sustainable Practices

In the corporate sector, companies like General Electric are designing products to enable their clients to compete in a carbon-constrained world. Novo Nordisk is taking a holistic view of combating diabetes not only through treatment but also through prevention. And Whole Foods and others are addressing the demand for quality food by sourcing local and organic produce. Importantly, the business response is about making money for shareholders, not altruism.

In the nongovernmental sector, organizations such as World Resources Institute, Transparency International, the Coalition for Environmentally Responsible Economies (CERES) and AccountAbility are helping companies explore how best to align corporate responsibility with business strategy.

---

*While we are seeing evidence of leading public companies adopting sustainable business practices in developed markets, there is still a long way to go.*

---

Over the past five years we have seen markets begin to incorporate the external cost of carbon dioxide emissions. This is happening through pricing mechanisms (price per ton of carbon dioxide) and government-supported trading platforms such as the European Union Emissions Trading Scheme in Europe. Even without a regulatory framework in the U.S., voluntary markets are emerging, such as the Chicago Climate Exchange and state-level initiatives such as the Regional Greenhouse Gas Initiative. These market mechanisms increasingly enable companies to calculate project returns and capital expenditures decisions with the price of carbon dioxide fully integrated.

The investment community has also started to respond. For example, the Enhanced Analytics Initiative, an international collaboration between asset owners and managers, encourages investment research that considers the impact of extra-financial issues on long-term company performance. The Equator Principles, designed to help financial institutions manage environmental and social risk in project financing, have now been adopted by 40 banks which arrange over 75% of the world's project loans. In addition, the rise in shareholder activism and the growing debate on fiduciary responsibility, governance legislation and reporting requirements (such as the Global Reporting Initiative and the EU Business Review) indicate the mainstream incorporation of sustainability concerns.

## A Long Way to Go

While we are seeing evidence of leading public companies adopting sustainable business practices in developed markets, there is still a long way to go to make sustainability fully integrated and therefore truly mainstream. A short-term focus still pervades both corporate and investment communities, which hinders long-term value creation.

As some have said, "We are operating the Earth like it's a business in liquidation." More mechanisms to incorporate environmental and social externalities will be needed to enable capital markets to achieve their intended purpose—to consistently allocate capital to its highest and best use for the good of the people and the planet.

# Free Trade Protects the Environment

## Global Freedom to Trade Campaign

*About the author: Global Freedom to Trade Campaign is a coalition of nongovernmental organizations that believes that freedom to trade is fundamental both for personal empowerment and development for all people in all countries.*

For years environmental groups have promoted the view that trade is bad for the environment. They argue that businesses want free trade so that they can escape regulations, and that trade leads to a "race to the bottom" for environmental standards. According to this view, corporations are causing poverty and environmental degradation. They want consumers in wealthy countries to feel guilty for consuming goods which were produced by people in developing countries. Such myths must be put to rest. . . .

## Environmental Problems in Poor Countries

The majority of environmental problems in poor countries are local: indoor air pollution, dirty water, and a lack of sanitation are the biggest environmental problems, leading to millions of people suffering from disease, and millions of premature deaths each year.

- Over 1 billion people lack access to clean drinking water.

- Over 2 billion people lack access to improved sanitation, and the majority of these people are in Africa and Asia, mostly in rural areas.

Global Freedom to Trade Campaign, "Freedom to Trade Protects the Environment," *Environment & Trade Briefing Paper*, August 2003. www.policynetwork.net/main/article.php?article_id=532.

- There are 4 billion cases of diarrhoea each year, resulting in 2.2 million deaths, most of them children under the age of five. "This is equivalent to one child dying every 15 seconds, or 20 jumbo jets crashing every day."

- "Indoor air [pollution] increases the risk of acute respiratory infections, [and is] one of the leading causes of infant and child mortality in developing countries. In Asia, such exposure accounts for between half and one million excess deaths every year. In sub-Saharan Africa the estimate is 300,000–500,000 excess deaths."

- Poor countries have often abandoned the needs of their poorest citizens, by adopting strategies and policies that make it more difficult for people to have access to clean water and sanitation, electricity, and technologies which would improve their lives.

- Dirty water and poor sanitation is a primary vehicle for poverty diseases.

- Water-borne diseases, including intestinal worms, guinea worms, schistosomiasis, trachoma, cholera, typhoid, hepatitis A, and dysentery, affect at least half a billion poor people.

- Another half-billion people are affected by water-related diseases, such as malaria and dengue fever.

- 2 billion people worldwide rely on biomass, including wood, dung, and crop residues, for cooking, heat, and light, mostly burned in poorly-flued indoor stoves. These are a primary source of indoor air pollution.

## Trade Helps to Eliminate Poverty

There is much sound evidence and no sound opposition, to the idea that "wealthier is healthier" and "wealthier is cleaner". The diseases of poor countries once plagued wealthy countries, but they were eliminated because of economic development. Health and development go hand in hand, and frustrating economic growth will only compromise the ability of countries to improve human health, adopt new technologies, afford better drugs and achieve improvements in healthcare that rich countries enjoy.

By allowing people to exchange without intervention, trade also means that people have more incentives to innovate and create new ways to solve problems.

Poverty means that people's priority is mere survival rather than protecting the environment. When incomes rise and people become wealthier, they can think about the future. It is then that they demand better environmental protection and use better technologies, such as more efficient fuels like gas and electricity, more efficient cars, and better sanitation, which lead to the saving of other resources and fewer local environmental problems.

## Trade Restrictions Stifle Development

Trade is the process by which people voluntarily exchange goods and services, which are produced with natural and human resources. People in poor countries have been restricted in their ability to trade, both by foreign countries through protectionist trade barriers, agricultural subsidies, and by their own governments, through protectionist trade barriers, corruption, a lack of property rights, and oppressive regulations. Free trade is an important step towards giving poor people access to external markets, and towards forcing corrupt governments to reform their policies.

Trade and exchange is fundamental to development, which then enables people to adopt higher standards for production. But to require the latter (regulations) before the former (development) will only prolong poverty. The effect of trade restrictions is to prevent voluntary exchange, and to replace it with regulations and restrictions enforced by the state.

Such restrictions are often motivated by economic interest groups who beg for government protection from external competition. Environmental groups seek to restrict trade on the basis that some goods produced by poor people do not meet the regulatory standards of wealthy countries, based on arbitrary criteria such as the "precautionary principle", or based on the fact that a country has not signed up to international environmental laws.

---

*While it may be an intuitively appealing argument that companies exploit resources and the environment in poor countries, it is false.*

---

## Five Myths About Trade and the Environment

*Myth*: Trade is a "race to the bottom" and leads to a reduction in environmental standards.

*Reality: Trade is beneficial for everyone. It leads to higher production standards, better use of resources, innovation and new technologies.*

While it may be an intuitively appealing argument that companies exploit resources and the environment in poor countries, it is false. Local producers in poor countries often have no choice but to use old production processes and goods which may use resources inefficiently and may cause environmental harms. The process of trade brings investment and better technologies which replace these, leading to more efficient use of resources.

Trade also leads to higher wages, and people may cease environmentally harmful activities because they shift into other professions, and because they can afford new technologies which are more environmentally benign.

*Myth*: Trade sanctions and restrictions lead to better environmental protection.

*Reality: Sanctions do not provide the right incentives for environmental protection, and may perversely lead to worse environmental consequences.*

Trade bans (sanctions) in international environmental agreements are not effective at achieving environmental goals and the same applies to environmental provisions in trade rules. Banning trade in certain goods, especially against producers in poor countries, does not mean that environmentally harmful production will cease. Rather, those producers will continue such activities, which largely take place in the informal economy. Those producers will remain poor and less able to replace old technologies with new ones, and less able to invest, thus environmentally harmful activities may continue.

Moreover, the value of some goods (wildlife and its products, for instance) is higher when trade is restricted or banned. This creates a perverse incentive to produce and sell that good (i.e. endangered species), rather than protect it. This is especially true when trade restrictions undermine the ability of poor people to control their own land and resources. Making trade illegal also means that trade in banned goods is not transparent, and it is thus more difficult to control. Regarding wildlife, "There have been remarkably few, if any, species extinctions that can be attributed to exploitation for international trade."

Trade sanctions could also drive up production costs, discouraging companies from investing and producing in poor countries—whether they are small local producers or multinationals. Moreover, trade sanctions distort prices, leading to less efficient uses of natural resources.

*Myth*: The process of trade leads to an unsustainable consumption of natural resources, dumping of wastes in poor countries, and contributes to global warming.

*Reality: Sustainable consumption results from wealth and trade, and poor people should be able to choose whatever lifestyle they desire, rather than having those choices imposed on them.*

Environmental groups seek regulations which would force people to consume fewer resources, and consume products which are made locally rather than transported, on the grounds that this is "sustainable" consumption. This makes little sense, though, as it would result in the overuse and exploitation of some resources, and underuse of others. Moreover, this may lead to different environmental problems—such as local air and water pollution.

---

*It is simply patronizing to suggest that people—whether poor or wealthy—should not be allowed to buy . . . products that improve their lives.*

---

By denying technology transfer and economic development that comes from open, rules-based trade, businesses and people in poor countries will continue to use technologies that cause harm to the environment and themselves. Without trade, investment and economic development, poor people would not use more efficient stoves or more efficient fuels. They would not use chlorine-based chemicals to rid their water of cholera, hepatitis and other deadly bacteria. If allowed to continue, environmental restrictions on trade could lead to more poverty.

It is simply patronizing to suggest that people—whether poor or wealthy—should not be allowed to buy cars (or refrigerators, hair dryers, lipstick and mobile phones), products that improve their lives, on the basis that this might cause environmental problems. The problems that poor people face currently are related to a lack of consumption of energy and resources, rather than too much of it.

*Myth*: Corporations and wealth cause poverty and environmental degradation, and government intervention is the only way to prevent this.

*Reality: Poverty, and resulting environmental problems, is caused by a lack of trade, investment, and supporting institu-*

tions. *Most poor country governments have prolonged this situation through restrictions on trade.*

The goal of businesses (whether local or foreign) is not to destroy the environment or to deplete resources. Business uses resources to fulfill consumers' needs and desires, through competition and prices. Involving government with trade encourages a system based on power and privilege, rather than on the best use of resources.

In essence, this simply perpetuates an existing situation in poor countries, where entrepreneurship is stifled, market access is restricted (both internally and externally), and the use of natural resources is decided with a political process—lobbying, bribery, corruption—rather than by individuals, consumers and actors in the market.

This system was formerly called mercantilism: "To achieve its objectives, the mercantilist state granted privileges to favored producers and consumers by means of regulations, subsidies, taxes and licenses." While a few people and businesses do benefit from mercantilism (or its modern equivalents), the majority of people are stifled by it and in poor countries it will perpetuate poverty.

*Myth*: Environmental regulations should take precedence over trade rules, and these should be harmonized and enforced by international agencies.

*Reality: If regulations are imposed on poor countries, it will slow their path of development and will prolong poverty.*

Environmental groups want to make international environmental rules superior to trade rules, and they want to "link" trade rules with environmental rules. Their goal is to stop trade which they deem to be environmentally harmful. Vested interests (such as businesses) support these measures because they can also be used as trade protectionism. The purpose of trade rules is to eliminate discrimination—either blatant or inherent.

[If] international regimes are used to impose environmental standards on poor countries, their poverty will be prolonged. Instead of focusing on the desires of environmental groups, poor countries should pursue a strategy to eliminate poverty. This means enabling everyone—not just corrupt politicians and the elite—to create, innovate, and build wealth. Free trade and the removal of onerous regulations which prevent exchange between people are two fundamental steps in this strategy.

---

*The best way to eliminate poverty and protect the environment is to encourage a regime of open trade.*

---

If specific environmental goals are deemed important enough to merit international action, then these policies should exist alongside trade agreements, without a need to make one or the other superior. The purpose of trade rules is to facilitate trade between people, and the purpose of environmental rules is to protect the environment. These are mutually supporting policies, because trade leads to wealth creation, which leads to better environmental protection.

## Open Trade will Lead to Better Environmental Protection

Regulations, trade restrictions, and less economic growth are not the best way to protect the environment, because they do not strike at the heart of environmental problems. "Environmental protection" has different meanings in wealthy and poor countries. In wealthy countries, it often means more government regulations and protection of endangered species, less intensive agriculture and 'renewable' energy.

To people in the developing world, such 'standards' are absurd: what matters to their well-being is access to clean water and sanitation, reliable energy sources, and access to technologies that will improve their productivity and help them to generate income, thus to escape poverty.

The best way to eliminate poverty *and* protect the environment is to encourage a regime of open trade along with other supporting policies. Freedom to trade is an important step towards eliminating poverty and towards better environmental protection.

# NAFTA's Environmental Protections Have Worked

## Gustavo Vega-Canovas

**About the author**: *Gustavo Vega-Canovas is a professor at the Center for International Studies at El Colegio de Mexico, Mexico City, Mexico, and was Associate Director of the Center for North American Studies at Duke University, 1998–1999.*

Mexico and the United States share both a long border and a long history of economic integration. Mexico is currently the United States' second largest trading partner after Canada, accounting approximately for ten to eleven percent of the United States' exports and imports. The United States, on the other hand, is Mexico's dominant trading partner, accounting for more than two-thirds of both imports and exports and far outdistancing Mexico's trade with Europe, Japan, the rest of Latin America, and Canada. The United States is also the major source of foreign investment flows in the Mexican economy, accounting for more than seventy percent of the total. Labor market integration is also very high. Mexican migrant labor has had a large impact on the United States economy by increasing the labor supply—an effect probably greater than that arising from increased United States-Mexican commodity trade, foreign investment or financial transactions. At least ten percent of the growth of the United States labor supply since World War II is due to Mexican migrants.

## Environmental Problems

Not all of the impacts of this deepening integration between both countries has been beneficial. In recent decades and especially since the inception of the Maquiladora program in the mid-sixties, the environment has become a highly charged

Gustavo Vega-Canovas, "NAFTA and the Environment," *Denver Journal of International Law and Policy*, Winter 2001, vol. 30, iss. 1, p. 55.

regional issue, particularly in urban clusters along the United States-Mexico border. Whether it is the dumping of raw sewage, over-irrigation, or overuse of fertilizers, environmental policies and practices in each country affect its neighbor. According to recent estimates, environmental conditions have worsened along the United States-Mexico border over the past decade. Explosive growth has created new jobs and raised incomes, but it has been accompanied by more pollution.

---

*[President Clinton negotiated an environmental agreement that] would not threaten to impose any significant costs on United States business enterprises.*

---

Worsening conditions in the environment along the United States-Mexico border date back to the 1970's and deteriorated even further during the "lost decade" of deep economic crisis in Mexico in the 1980's. It shouldn't be surprising that the proposal to deepen economic integration through a North American Free Trade Agreement (NAFTA) provoked such a sharp opposition from the environmental community in the United States. According to environmental groups, the increased industrial growth that NAFTA would produce would further deteriorate Mexico's environmental infrastructure, lax enforcement of environmental laws would encourage "environmental dumping" and increased competition would provoke a "race to the bottom," a weakening of environmental standards in all three countries. They demanded that any trade agreements should include strong safeguards against real or potential abuses.

NAFTA was initially opposed by most major United States environmental groups, and environmental group opposition was a significant factor influencing opposition by many Democratic members of the United States Congress. From the onset of NAFTA negotiations, Democratic members of Congress pressed the Republican administration of past-President

George Bush, senior, to make NAFTA more environment-friendly, and the Bush administration negotiated some basic provisions protective of the environment with the governments of Canada and Mexico.

As part of his presidential campaign, past-President William Clinton proposed the negotiation of supplemental agreements on the environment and labor. When President Clinton entered office . . . [he] chose to negotiate two supplemental agreements which gave the impression of addressing environmental and labor concerns, but which would not threaten to impose any significant costs on United States business enterprises. Clinton also chose not to spend large sums of federal money on improving conditions in United States and Mexican border communities. In the absence of a United States commitment to a regional bank, Canada and Mexico preferred a less confrontational approach to dealing with environmental issues in the region and did not agree to key United States demands, particularly enforcement provisions. Thus, the NAFTA side accord on environment did not deliver on some of Clinton's ambitious environmental promises. Such a situation has meant that major environmental groups which initially supported NAFTA and the parallel side agreements have become increasingly dissatisfied with government efforts to deal with environmental issues in the region and have since opposed new trade initiatives.

Do the . . . years since NAFTA and the parallel side agreements went into effect, justify the criticisms of environmental groups? This paper attempts to respond to this question by analyzing the terms of the North American Agreement on Environmental Cooperation (NAAEC) and its implementation history. . . .

## THE NAAEC

The NAAEC was created to establish a "framework . . . to facilitate effective cooperation on the conservation, protection and enhancement of the environment" and set up an institution, the North American Commission for Environmental Cooperation (CEC) to facilitate joint activities and mediate environmental disputes.

Part 1 of the NAAEC comprises an ambitious set of objectives including the protection and improvement of the environment, the promotion of sustainable development, and enhanced compliance with and enforcement of environmental laws. Part 2 imposes on the parties to periodically issue reports on the state of their environment, to develop environmental emergency preparedness measures, to promote environmental education, to develop environmental technology and scientific research; to assess environmental impacts; and to "ensure that [their] laws and regulations provide for high levels of environmental protection."

---

*The NAAEC parties are not subject to specific requirements in terms of environmental protection.*

---

Part 3 of the NAAEC establishes the CEC with three components: the Council; the Secretariat; and, the Joint Public Advisory Committee (JPAC). The Council consists of the three environment ministers of the parties, and is the executive decision-making body of the CEC. The Secretariat serves at the direction of the Council and its officials are independent of the party governments. The NAAEC establishes an inter-party dispute settlement mechanism that permits claims based on an allegation of persistent failure to enforce environmental laws. A party that is found to have consistently failed to enforce such laws is expected to devise and implement an "action plan" to remedy this situation. If an action plan is not accepted or implemented, a monetary fine may be imposed on the recalcitrant party. The maximum fine is a modest amount and it is to be expended at the direction of the Council to remedy the situation of non-compliance in the defaulting party.

In addition to the inter-party dispute settlement mechanism, private parties (including interest groups) may file petitions with the Secretariat requesting the preparation of a "factual record." If certain threshhold requirements are determined by the Secretariat to be met, the Secretariat will request the Council to authorize the preparation of a factual record. The Council may approve the recommendation to prepare a factual record by a two-thirds vote. The Secretariat is responsible for developing and preparing the factual record, and submitting it to the Council. The Council may approve the publication of the factual record by a two thirds-vote.

## The NAAEC Implementation History

When one carefully studies the different provisions of the NAAEC and takes into account its implementation history so far, several observations can be made:

First, the NAAEC parties are not subject to specific requirements in terms of environmental protection. Each party is free to determine its own level of protection and to modify its rules. In other words, this main substantive obligation was deliberately drafted to be imprecise. It was clear to all governments involved in the negotiations that the US was not seeking an agreement which would impose significant compliance obligations.

The Secretariat may prepare and publish a "factual record". The publication of a factual record serves a transparency and publicity function. While NAAEC governments may alter their behavior based on adverse publicity, there is no legal obligation that arises from the publication of an adverse factual record. Intergovernmental dispute settlement in the context of the NAAEC is limited to claims that a party has persistently failed to enforce its environmental laws. This standard has been difficult and will be difficult to apply. Only in rare circumstances do governments persistently enforce their laws, relying instead on voluntary compliance by most persons. It shouldn't be a surprise therefore, that so far there have been no initiatives regarding persistent failure to enforce environmental law, and hence this mechanism remains untested.

Second, the NAAEC did not mean to change and has resulted in little change in the identity of persons who make environment-related decisions in the country-parties. Political decisions relating to the environment in each country-party continue to be made by the relevant authorities responsible for the environment before the NAAEC entered into force.

---

*The CEC [North American Commission for Environmental Cooperation] has managed ... to produce some change in intergovernmental conduct.*

---

The NAAEC has facilitated some interaction among NAFTA governments in respect to environmental matters. Representatives of the governments meet together on a regular basis in various NAAEC fora. The NAAEC institutions have had success in establishing a range of research and cooperation programs with respect to the North American environment. The CEC in particular has developed specific programs and project implementation in five priority areas: Pollutants and Health, Environment, Trade and the Economy, Environmental Conservation, Enforcement, [and] Information and Public Outreach.

## The NAAEC Has Helped Environmental Groups Influence Government Policy

Even though the CEC was devised not to effect any change in the way environmental policy is carried out in the three countries, the CEC has managed nevertheless to produce some change in intergovernmental conduct in developing ... reports of which the CEC has produced 3 so far. Of these three, the most significant has been the investigation of the death of migratory birds in the Silva Reservoir in Mexico, which concluded that Mexico was not responsible for the problem. A scientific panel identified specific actions to deal with the issue, but the final CEC recommendation to the Mexican government was only to conduct a comprehensive evaluation and propose solutions. As a result of the Silva report, an action program for the State of Guanajuato was developed, the state's first environmental council was created, and workshops on the Turbio River and waste-water treatment were established.

It is interesting to note that this report was a result of a petition filed with the CEC by the National Audubon Society [and two Mexican interest groups]. . . . The results of the case seem to suggest that in a broad sense the NAAEC appears to have enhanced the capacity of domestic interest groups to engage national government decision-makers in international relations. The capacity of environmental groups afforded by the NAAEC to internationalize the Silva Reservoir problem may have facilitated a more satisfactory investigation and report on the incident than would have been forthcoming in the absence of the CEC. Without the CEC, the matter would likely have been pursued through charges and countercharges between Mexican government authorities and NGOs [nongovernmental organizations], played out before the press. Significantly, the CEC provided a mechanism by which a major United States-based environmental organization was able to coordinate an investigation in Mexican territory with the cooperation of the Mexican government. Prior to the establishment of the CEC structure, it is doubtful that the National Audubon Society would have been able to pressure the United States Environmental Protection Agency . . . to persuade the Mexican government to allow a trilateral team of scientists to investigate the incident.

The NAAEC may have altered political relations between Mexico and the U.S. by providing a framework in which the EPA could more legitimately claim to examine Mexico's international governance. Also at the domestic level, it seems unlikely that the Mexican government would have responded seriously to a petition from Mexican environmental interest groups absent the internationalization of the incident.

# Free Trade Will Not Hurt the Environment if Trade Agreements Are Accompanied by Environmental Standards

*Nathan Johnson*

**About the author**: *Nathan Johnson is a third-year undergraduate at the College of William & Mary, majoring in economics and applied mathematics.*

## Environmentalism and the FTAA

The primary concern of the environmental lobbies is that further trade liberalization through the Free Trade Area of the Americas (FTAA) initiative [a trade agreement that would cover most of the western hemisphere] will have adverse consequences on the environment. Their first point is that international trade law under World Trade Organization (WTO) regulations provides an incentive to lower domestic environmental regulations, so that domestic producers will be on a "level playing field" with foreign competitors. The second concern is that the General Agreement on Tariffs and Trade (GATT) policy of "product, not process" prohibits the discrimination of imports based solely on the methods of production, a practice which induces foreign producers to use the cheapest (and environmentally costly) processes, knowing that their products will receive equal treatment as those made with "environmentally-friendly" production techniques.

The first question in evaluating the lobbyists' contentions is to determine to what extent trade liberalization has negative implications for the environment—is it really something we should worry about? And if so, what needs to be done to en-

Nathan Johnson, "Does Freer Trade Mean Lower Environmental Standards?" About, Inc., 2006. http://economics.about.com/cs/development/a/freer_trade.htm.

sure a global community that promotes both international trade and environmental preservation?

The integration of the world economy and the imperative to protect the environment are two of the most powerful global trends that have emerged in recent decades. These forces have produced a conflict of interest between free-traders and environmentalists, as their advancements are commonly viewed as mutually exclusive. Environmental groups show a growing concern over the FTAA initiative, fearful that multinational corporations will move their production facilities to South America where the environmental regulations are less stringent. They claim that the WTO's refusal to implement environmental policies will lead to a "race to the bottom" in environmental standards among nations. Specifically, the Sierra Club argues that "the FTAA could have a severe impact on our health and environment at home and throughout the Americas. It could expose more of our health and environmental laws to attack as trade barriers and encourage destructive mining and logging in some of our hemisphere's most precious wild areas".

The aforementioned concerns are legitimate and theoretically sound. Firms want to produce where they have lower costs of production, and avoiding pollution reduction techniques is a cost saver. Domestically, producers could claim foreign production facilities and firms have an unfair advantage because of lower environmental standards, so business lobbies would pressure for lower domestic standards in an effort to stay "competitive" with goods produced abroad. One of the most famous examples of international trade policy under the GATT colliding with domestic environmental policy is the tuna-dolphin dispute between the U.S. and Mexico.

## The Tuna-Dolphin Dispute

In 1991, the U.S. imposed trade restrictions on Mexico and several other countries because of their excessive byproduct dolphin kill by tuna fishermen, levels above those allowed by the U.S. Marine Mammal Protection Act of 1972. Mexico and its allies appealed to a GATT dispute settlement panel, claiming unfair trade practices. The U.S. cited Article 20 as justification for its ban, which provides for exceptions "necessary to protect human, animal, or plant life or health". The GATT panel upheld Mexico's challenge, saying that the United States' embargo violated the GATT's non-discrimination policy among member nations, as the Mexican process of tuna fishing did not result in a differentiated product from other exporters. It found that the embargo was not "necessary," as the U.S. had claimed, to protecting "human, animal, or plant life or health," and also that the U.S. had not exhausted other less trade-restrictive remedies. Failure of the necessity test suggested that there were other options the U.S. had overlooked in solving the tuna-dolphin problem.

---

*Something must be done to ensure that trade liberalization is accompanied by appropriate environmental policy.*

---

In 1990, three major U.S. canneries announced that they would only sell tuna that was caught with dolphin safe methods. Labeling their products as dolphin safe became a way to differentiate the product by the process, by appealing to consumers' desires to purchase dolphin safe tuna. Then in 1992, 10 countries (including the U.S. and Mexico) adopted the La Jolla Agreement, which established an international limit on dolphin mortality rates among tuna fishers. From 1989 to 1993, dolphin deaths declined from nearly 100,000 to 3,600, an impressive drop made possible through international negotiations.

On the other side of the issue, free-traders like Paul Krugman argue that there is little reason to insist on global environmental standards, as doing so could diminish the gains from trade. Krugman correctly notes that, "international trade is really just a production technique, a way to produce importables indirectly by first producing exportables, then exchanging them." He then goes on to add, that "it does not matter from the point of view of the national gains from trade whether other countries have different relative prices because they have different resources, different technologies or different environmental standards. All that matters is that they be different then we can gain from trading with them." While theoretically correct, Krugman's argument carries the implicit assumption that the U.S. is a rational actor whose sole aim is maximizing national gains from trade. In the real world, this assumption is not plausible. We know from experience that for whatever reasons, many Americans do have an (apparently economically "irrational") interest in preserving the Amazon or protecting endangered species in China. In this era of globalization, the benefits of liberalization must be carefully weighed with the environmental costs, in an effort to produce a socially optimal equilibrium. Krugman is accurate in saying that uniform harmonization of environmental standards is inappropriate, as different countries have different pollution problems and varying valuations of environmental damage. However, something must be done to ensure that trade liberalization is accompanied by appropriate environmental policy.

## Environmental Impact of Trade Liberalization

We must certainly lend credence to evidence that suggests liberalizing trade can hurt the environment. But before proposing a solution, it is necessary to examine when trade hurts and when it in fact helps the environment. Trade without accompanying environmental policy hurts the environment when it induces an increase in environmentally costly production processes. Take for example a small country that . . . produces both sugar and rice. For whatever reason, rice production has a negative externality of soil erosion. Now assume that on the global market this country has a comparative advantage in rice production. Opening up its markets will allow the country to export rice and import sugar based on comparative advantage. The downside to this ... is that the country is now producing more rice, which leads to further soil erosion, making the environment worse off. The overall effect on the country's national welfare is ambiguous, depending on whether or not the gains from trade outweigh the social cost of soil erosion. ...

---

*Opening markets to trade and preserving the environment are equally desirable goals.*

---

Now assume that this same country has a comparative advantage in sugar production. In this case liberalization will allow the country to export sugar and import rice, which cuts down on soil erosion. This scenario leads to a net benefit to the global environment, as rice farming is moved to locations that can presumably do it with less soil erosion. Here the national welfare effect is also unambiguously positive. Another potential environmental benefit of liberalization in developing economies is that they will see faster economic growth and be endowed with the resources to take appropriate environmental measures. The technology that Western firms use to reduce pollution would become more readily available to many South American countries if the FTAA goes into effect.

## Trade Agreements Reinforced By Environmental Protections

In order to develop rational policy suggestions, we must realize that opening markets to trade and preserving the environment are equally desirable goals. A principle of economic planning put forth by Nobel Laureate Jan Tinbergen is that each target of economic policy (in this case free trade and the environment) warrants a separate instrument aimed at it. So while environmental problems may be reinforced by trade policy, they are best resolved by environmental policy. This principle suggests the need for mutually reinforcing trade and environmental agreements between countries, which often involves tradeoffs. Sensible policy tradeoffs include "slightly less agriculture output in return for cleaner water; slightly more erosion in return for farm exports and income". In practice, such arrangements were provided for in the environmental side agreement that was included in the North American Free Trade Agreement (NAFTA). This agreement insisted that the member countries adhere to certain environmental standards, and saw the formation of the trilateral Commission on Environmental Cooperation, which had the authority to oversee and enforce these regulations.

NAFTA has not created many of the environmental problems that critics had predicted. In fact, its implementation and the debate surrounding it have increased environmental awareness not only in the U.S. but in Mexico as well, which has adopted higher environmental standards since the treaty's inception. With regard to the FTAA concerns by the environmental lobbyists, the likelihood that U.S. domestic environmental policy will be relaxed due to foreign competitors is quite low. The United States is simply too large to be heavily affected by South American producers gaining a slightly larger market share. However, there is a legitimate concern that firms will try to take advantage of lax environmental standards in South American countries.

In order to address this possibility, the U.S. should take the lead in drafting environmental legislation to accompany the FTAA, as it did with NAFTA. Specifically, it should outline environmental standards that are to be met by the member countries at certain dates. . . . When this is done, North and South America will be able to take full advantage of trade opportunities, and the benefits will not have to come at the cost of the world's environment.

CHAPTER 4

# Is Globalization a Threat to Democracy?

# Chapter Preface

Part of the debate over globalization is about how the phenomenon will affect national governments around the world. Some commentators believe, for example, that global trade, communications, and transportation will help democracy to sprout in countries with histories of authoritarian rule. Global activities, they argue, expose people living under repressive regimes to demand democratic ideas and freedoms, thereby lessening the control of dictators and creating new opportunities for political dissent.

For those who see globalization as a possible boon for democracy, China poses a critical test for their theory. Since 1949, The People's Republic of China has been ruled by a Communist dictatorship, first under Mao Zedong, then under Deng Xiaoping, followed by Jiang Zemin until his retirement in 2002. Today, a new generation of Chinese leaders has taken the reins of power, led by President Hu Jintao. Under China's system of government, there is only one political party—the Chinese Communist Party—and it makes all critical political, economic, and social decisions. Most institutions, even the media, are state-controlled and citizens have no political freedoms or civil rights. Those who protest or dissent from Communist Party policies are subjected to sometimes brutal repression. In the spring of 1989, for example, the Chinese government sent out tanks and troops to suppress a political demonstration in Tiananmen Square in the Chinese capital of Beijing—an action that resulted in the massacre of thousands of unarmed citizens.

In recent years, however, Chinese leaders have embraced free trade policies and technologies in an attempt to improve China's economy; this decision brought the country rapid economic growth but also opened Chinese society to outside influences. Today, an increasing number of Chinese citizens are able to travel, interact with Westerners, obtain foreign educations, and use new communication technologies. These changes have provided a window to the United States and the rest of the world and have exposed many Chinese to democratic concepts such as free elections and the right to free speech, press, religion, and association. China's leaders continue to try to suppress political dissent but it is becoming increasingly difficult, resulting in a tug-of-war between authorities and globalization forces.

China's experience with the Internet is one of the most interesting aspects of the social and political tensions created by globalization. As of 2006, only a small percent of Chinese have Internet access, but because China's population is so large, that constitutes over 150 million Internet users—as many or more than there are in the United States. Moreover, this number is growing at a rate of 400 percent per year. Also, according to the China Internet Network Information Center (CNNIC), close to 70 percent of this Internet usage time is spent looking at news sites, demonstrating a voracious Chinese appetite for uncensored political information. Many commentators predict the Internet will lead to more political dissent and force the Chinese government to become less authoritarian.

Chinese leaders, however, have waged a determined war to keep citizens from using the Internet for political purposes. Today, the government registers all Internet users, regulates what topics may be discussed online, and invests heavily in technology to monitor and filter Internet communications. Often called the "Great Firewall," this government censorship program is highly sophisticated and employs a force of at least 30,000 Internet police to filter foreign Web sites, monitor local Web addresses, and censor blogs, online chat rooms, and instant messages. All Internet traffic entering or leaving China must travel through nine government gateways, where politically offensive content is promptly removed. As newspaper reporter Benjamin Joffe-Walt wrote in 2005 in *The Guardian*, "Banned phrases . . . include independence, democracy, . . . Tiananmen Square, [and] freedom." Citizens who violate these censorship rules often end up in jail. In September 2005, for example, a Chinese journalist and former professor who wrote articles for banned foreign Web sites was given a seven-year sentence for "inciting subversion."

Ironically, China has managed to develop this huge censorship program only with the help of U.S. Internet technology companies. Much of the technology used for the "Great Firewall" reportedly came from an American company, Cisco Systems; Microsoft agreed to censor the content on its blog service; and the two major search engine companies, Yahoo and Google, have both capitulated to China's censorship policies in order to do business in the country. Yahoo even provided Chinese authorities with information that led to the 2005 arrest and sentencing of the journalist.

Despite these strenuous censorship efforts, committed hackers, constant advances in technology, and the sheer growth of the Internet still threaten to overwhelm the Chinese government's attempt to control online political dissent. As *New York Times* columnist Nicolas Kristof concluded in a 2005 column, "There just aren't enough police to control the Internet." In response to the growing threat, Chinese President Hu Jintao in 2005 called for a new crackdown on Internet usage—what he called a "smokeless war" against "liberal elements" in China. In early 2006, Chinese authorities even suggested that China will create its own Chinese domain names. Such a system could free Chinese Internet users from using the dot-com and dot-net domain names managed by the U.S.-based Internet Corporation for Assigned Names and Numbers (ICANN), the system now uniformly used around the globe. Some experts worry this could mark the end of a truly free and global Internet.

Although China has since claimed that it has no plans to split off from the Internet, any increased government control over the Internet in China does not bode well for Internet-led political reform. The outcome of the Chinese struggle is therefore still uncertain, and as the following viewpoints illustrate, the debate over globalization's effects on the power of national governments continues.

# Global Capitalism Is Subverting Democracy

*Noreen Hertz*

**About the author***: Noreen Hertz is an economist from the United Kingdom's University of Cambridge who once worked for the World Bank. Hertz is the author of the book,* The Silent Takeover: Global Capitalism and the Death of Democracy *(2004), from which the following viewpoint is excerpted as a modified and edited version.*

Corporations have become behemoths, huge global giants that wield immense political power. Propelled by government policies of privatization, deregulation, and trade liberalization, and the technological developments of the past twenty years, a power shift has taken place. The hundred largest multinational corporations now control about 20 percent of global foreign assets, and fifty-one of the one hundred biggest economies in the world are now corporations. The sales of General Motors and Ford are greater than the GDP of the whole of sub-Saharan Africa; the assets of IBM, BP, and General Electric outstrip the economic capabilities of most small nations; and Wal-Mart, the supermarket retailer, has higher revenues than most Central and Eastern Europe states.

## The Growth of Corporations

The size of corporations is increasing. In the first year of the new millennium, Vodafone merged with Mannesmann (a purchase worth $183 billion), Chrysler with Daimler (the merged company now employs over 400,000 people), Smith Kline Beecham with Glaxo Wellcome (now reporting pretax profits of $7.6 billion as Glaxo-SmithKline), and AOL with Time Warner in a merger worth $350 billion—five thousand merg-

Noreen Hertz, *The Silent Takeover: Global Capitalism and the Death of Democracy.* New York: The Free Press, 2004, pp. 6–12.

ers in total in 2000, and double the level of a decade earlier. These megamergers mock the M&A activity of the 1980s. Each new merger is bigger than the one before, and governments rarely stand in the way. Each new merger gives corporations even more power. All the goods we buy or use—our gasoline, the drugs our doctors prescribe, essentials like water, transport, health, and education, even the new school computers and the crops growing in the fields around our communities—are in the grip of corporations which may, at their whim, nurture, support, or strangle us.

---

*Never before in modern times has the gap between the haves and the have-nots been so wide.*

---

This is the world of the Silent Takeover, the world at the dawn of the new millennium. Governments' hands appear tied and we are increasingly dependent on corporations. Business is in the driver's seat, corporations determine the rules of the game, and governments have become referees, enforcing rules laid down by others. Portable corporations are now movable feasts and governments go to great lengths to attract or retain them on their shores. Blind eyes are turned to tax loopholes. Business moguls use sophisticated tax dodges to keep their bounty offshore. [Australian billionaire] Rupert Murdoch's News Corporation pays only 6 percent tax worldwide; and in the U.K., up to the end of 1998, it paid no net British corporation tax at all, despite having made £1.4 billion [$2.6 billion] profit there since June 1987. This is a world in which, although we already see the signs of the eroding tax base in our crumbling public services and infrastructure, our elected representatives kowtow to business, afraid not to dance to the piper's tune.

Governments once battled for physical territory; today they fight in the main for market share. One of their primary jobs has become that of ensuring an environment in which business can prosper, and which is attractive to business. The role of nation states has become to a large extent simply that of providing the public goods and infrastructure that business needs at the lowest costs while protecting the world's free trade system.

## The Increasing Gap Between Haves and Have-Nots

In the process, justice, equity, rights, the environment, and even issues of national security fall by the wayside. Take the case of the Taliban—supported by the United States until 1997 because of U.S. oil company interests, despite the regime's dismal human rights record. Social justice has come to mean access to markets. Social safety nets have been weakened. Union power has been smashed.

Never before in modern times has the gap between the haves and the have-nots been so wide, never have so many been excluded or so championless. Forty-five million Americans have no health insurance. In Manhattan, people fish empty drink cans and bottles from trash cans to claim their five cents' redemption value, while in London, car windshield washers armed with squeegees and pails of dirty water ambush drivers at traffic lights. Americans spend $8 billion a year on cosmetics while the world cannot find the $9 billion the UN reckons is needed to give all people access to clean drinking water and sanitation. The British Labour party has gone on record as saying that wealth creation is now more important than wealth redistribution.

In America, during the ten years after 1988, income for the poorest families rose less than 1 percent, while it jumped 15 percent for the richest fifth. In New York City the poorest 20 percent earn an annual average of $10,700 while the wealthiest 20 percent earn $152,350. Wages for those at the bottom are so low that, despite the country's low unemployment figures, millions of employed Americans and one in five

American children are now living in poverty. Never since the 1920s has the gap between rich and poor been so great. Bill Gates's net worth alone at the end of the last century, for example, equaled the total net worth of the bottom 50 percent of American families.

Capitalism has triumphed, but its spoils are not shared by all. Its failings are ignored by governments which, thanks to the very policy measures they introduced, are increasingly unable to deal with the consequences of their system.

## Fading Political Systems

And that system is rotten. Political scandals are unveiled all too frequently: ... even those politicians not on the take are increasingly indebted to or enmeshed with business.

Nowhere is this more apparent than in the United States. [Bill] Clinton's presidency was immersed in scandal at once: from the Whitewater allegations, via overnight stays in the Lincoln bedroom for party funders, to the final act of pardoning tax evader and arms dealer Marc Rich. For candidates for the 2000 American presidential elections, their very ability to run depended upon their securing corporate funding. George W. Bush's campaign war chest was $191 million, [Al] Gore's $133 million. And objections to the McCain-Feingold bill on campaign finance reform, which once in effect would ban businesses, trade unions, and individuals from making unlimited "soft money" contributions to American political parties, came from both Democrats and Republicans.

No wonder the politicians' star is fading. People recognize politicians' conflicting interests and unwillingness to champion them, and are beginning to abandon politics en masse. Whereas the 1980s saw democracy emerging all over the world as the dominant mode of government, imbued with a unique legitimacy and commanding mass support, by the 1990s voter turnout almost everywhere was falling, party membership declining, and politicians rated below meter maids as worthy of respect. All over the world, from the old democracies of the United States and Western Europe to the young nations of Latin America and the Far East, people have less confidence in the institutions of government today than they had a decade ago. Only 59 percent of British voters voted at the 2001 general election, down from 69 percent in 1997, the lowest turnout since World War I. In the USA, not in nearly two centuries have so many American citizens freely abstained from voting as in the past six years. The product sold by politicians is seen as broken, no longer deemed worth buying. . . .

## A Critical Juncture

Over the last two decades the balance of power between politics and commerce has shifted radically, leaving politicians increasingly subordinate to the colossal economic power of big business. Unleashed by the [Ronald] Reagan—[Margaret] Thatcher axis, and accelerated by the end of the cold war, this process has grown hydralike over the last two decades and now manifests itself in what are diverse positive and negative forms. Whichever way we look at it, corporations are taking on the responsibilities of government.

---

*The steady erosion of government and politics is dangerous for us all, regardless of political persuasion.*

---

And as business has extended its role, it has . . . actually come to define the public realm. The political state has become the corporate state. Governments, by not even acknowledging the takeover, risk shattering the implicit contract between state and citizen that lies at the heart of a democratic society, making the rejection of the ballot box and the embracing of nontraditional forms of political expression increasingly attractive alternatives. . . .

We stand today at a critical juncture. If we do nothing, if we do not challenge the Silent Takeover, do not question our belief system, do not admit our own culpability in the creation of this "new world order," then all is lost. . . . Inequality of income is bad not only for the poor, but for the rich, too. The steady erosion of government and politics is dangerous for all regardless of political persuasion. A world in which George W. [Bush] passes law after law favoring the interests of big business, Rupert Murdoch [Australian billionaire and media CEO] has more power than Tony Blair [Britain's Prime Minister], and corporations set the political agenda is frightening and undemocratic. The idea of corporations taking over the roles of government might in some ways seem appealing, but risks leaving us increasingly without recourse.

# Globalization Presents a Serious Challenge to Democratic Sovereignty and the Democratic Nation-State

*John Fonte*

**About the author**: *John Fonte is director of the Center for American Common Culture and a senior fellow at the Hudson Institute, a conservative policy research organization dedicated to research and analysis that promotes global security, prosperity, and freedom.*

Just before the new century began, Marc Plattner, co-editor of the influential *Journal of Democracy*, wrote of the brave new globalized world coming into existence:

> A borderless world is unlikely to be a democratic one. For while the idea of "world citizenship" may sound appealing in theory, it is very hard to imagine it working successfully in practice. Indeed, some aspects of globalization, "point to a long range danger to democracy." . . .

An entire industry of transnational agencies and nongovernmental organizations is pushing forward changes designed either to deny or override the national sovereignty of democratic states against surprisingly muted or inchoate opposition. Taken together, these changes amount to a serious political and intellectual challenge to democratic sovereignty vested in the liberal democratic nation-state. . . . The 21st century could well turn out to be not the democratic century, but the "post-democratic" century—the century in which liberal democracy as we know it is slowly, almost imperceptibly, replaced by a new form of global governance.

John Fonte, "Democracy's Trojan Horse," *The National Interest*, Summer 2004, iss. 76, p. 117.

## The Global Governance Regime

The ideology and institutions already exist in embryonic form and are developing rapidly. The philosophical basis for global governance begins with the premise that all individuals on the planet possess human rights. International law is the paramount authority that determines those rights, while international agreements establish and expand new rights and norms. International institutions (for example, the UN, the International Criminal Court and the World Bank) monitor, adjudicate, negotiate, cajole and administer the international agreements and laws in varying degrees. International nongovernmental organizations (NGOs) claim to represent "global civil society", or the "peoples" of the planet. And the NGOs work with international institutions and participate in international conferences helping develop the new norms for global governance. Moreover, global governance is not really "international", but "transnational" in the sense that it is not concerned strictly with relations between nations, but with political arrangements above and beyond nation-states. Indeed, it could also be described as "post-international."

The global governance regime is promoted and run by complementary and interlocking networks of transnational (mostly Western) elites including international lawyers, international judges, NGO activists, UN and other international organization officials, global corporate leaders, and some sympathetic officials and bureaucrats from nation-states. These transnational elites are, for the most part, ideologically compatible. They could be described as "transnational progressives" ... supporting what they perceive as "progressive" causes across national boundaries. ... Denationalized corporate elites who are non-ideological, but seek economic advantage, often have a symbiotic relationship with the transnational progressives. ... Nation-states (both democratic and undemocratic) continue to exist, but their authority is increasingly circumscribed by the growing strength of the global institutions, laws, rules, networks and ideological norms noted above.

Unlike democratic sovereignty, global governance can provide no straightforward answers to the most important questions of political science (Who governs?, Where does authority reside? How is legislation enacted?). In a democracy, authority resides in a self-constituted people. . . . These self-governing people choose their rulers through elections and can replace them if they are not responsive to the people. The people limit the power of rulers through a constitution and basic laws. Bad laws can be changed by elected national legislatures.

In theory, human rights and international law are the moral basis for the global governance regime, but both of these concepts are fluid, porous and constantly "evolving." They are, at any given moment, what transnational elites tell us they are. NGOs participate in the writing of global treaties alongside democratic and non-democratic governments, but they are essentially pressure groups, elected by no one and responsible only to themselves. Nor are the other elites, the international lawyers, judges, activists and officials who participate in the global governance system responsible or accountable to any self-governing "people." How can these rulers be replaced? How can "the governed" repeal bad laws and regulations that their "governors" have imposed upon them? Global governance provides no democratic answers to these questions. . . .

## Global Governance in Action

Two major NGOs, Human Rights Watch and Amnesty International USA, are exemplars of the conflict between democracy and post-democracy. These two organizations have waged what could be characterized as "lawfare" against the exercise of democratic sovereignty by the American nation-state. They continuously pillory America's liberal democracy as an "oppressive" regime that routinely violates human rights.

Immediately following the attacks of September 11, they objected to describing the conflict as a "war", preferring to characterize them as a "crime" that should be pursued under the auspices of international law. As American planes began bombing the Taliban in Afghanistan in October 2001, the NGOs sought ways to limit American military operations by complaining about possible collateral damage and the use of weapons of which they do not approve, such as cluster bombs.

---

*The NGOs [nongovernmental organizations] believe that if international human rights laws and U.S. laws are in conflict, international laws supersede U.S. laws.*

---

Again and again, the NGOs have charged that civilian deaths in Afghanistan and Iraq could have been prevented by the U.S. military. For example, the HRW [Human Rights Watch] website condemned air strikes aimed at Saddam Hussein and other Iraqi leaders because they resulted in a small number of civilian deaths. HRW admitted they did not try to find the exact numbers of civilian deaths and retorted that, "focusing on the exact number of deaths misses the point. The point is the U.S. military should not have been using these methods of warfare."

It is important to note that the NGO attack is not simply opposition to the policies of the Bush Administration. America was also pilloried during the Clinton era as a "persistent" violator of human rights and international law. . . .

The NGOs believe that if international human rights laws and U.S. laws are in conflict, international laws supersede U.S. laws, even though these international laws have not been approved or enacted into American law by the relevant legislative bodies (Congress or a state legislature) through the normal processes of American constitutional democracy. . . .

Take, for example, the Convention on the Elimination of All Forms of Discrimination Against Women (CEDAW).

CEDAW has not been ratified by the Senate, even though Senators Joseph Biden (D-DE) and Barbara Boxer (D-CA) have argued that the treaty is simply an "international bill of rights" for women. But the experience of Britain and other democracies with CEDAW is quite illuminating.

*International organizations including the UN [United Nations] and its related agencies assist in the promotion of new structures of post-democratic governance.*

The British were told to "reconsider" their Sex Discrimination Act "in light" of CEDAW and implement gender preferences or quotas, euphemistically described as "temporary special measures." They were also told that the UK's Equal Pay Act was "outdated", because it did not employ "the vast amount of research in the United States on equal pay for work of equal value" or "comparable worth." Furthermore, they were told that to get men to take parental leave on a rate of parity with women, "forceful measures were sometimes needed." In 1999 the UN Committee monitoring Britain expressed "concern" that the percentage of women in Parliament was too low....

CEDAW is not simply an "international bill of rights for women"—as its adherents claim. Surely, questions of parental leave, the cost of contraceptives, day-care policy, gender parity in Parliament, and sensitivity training for police are issues that liberal democracies can work out for themselves. Missing in the CEDAW treaty is any concept of "government by consent of the governed."

## Symbiotic Relationships Between NGOs and International Organizations

While the evolving concepts of human rights and the "new" international law provide the ideology, NGOs supply the interest groups and activists, and international agreements the regulatory framework. At the same time, international organizations including the UN [United Nations] and its related agencies assist in the promotion of new structures of post-democratic governance. What Professor Kenneth Anderson has called a "symbiotic relationship" exists among the UN, its agencies, the NGOs, human rights lawyers and the international law community. The transnational elites and their activist allies are part of the same networks, share the same ideological predispositions and have similar material interests . . . in strengthening transnational institutions and norms at the expense of the institutions and laws of liberal democratic nation-states.

This is why they agree that the UN is the "sole source of legitimacy" for deciding when a democratic nation state can use force; promote unelected NGOs as representatives of "global civil society" in an attempt to create a type of democratic legitimacy that they do not possess; and work to strengthen the "new" international law and intrusive international agreements that transfer power (even on domestic issues) from democratically elected governments to transnational authorities.

---

*It was . . . rather unseemly for the corporate counsel of Motorola to denounce as "nationalistic" Ralph Nader's suggestion that American-based corporations begin their stockholder meetings with "The Pledge of Allegiance."*

---

## The Threat to Democracy

What does the challenge of post-democracy mean philosophically for the advance of genuine democracy in the world? . . . This alternative regime would consist of networks of overlapping transnational institutions, organizations, agreements, treaties, laws, regulations, and rules; run by transnational elites and informed by a transnational progressive ideology. This ideology is an amorphous and eclectic mix of soft academic

Marxism, . . . social democracy, . . . multiculturalism, radical feminism, environmentalism, or whatever else constitutes the latest in progressive thought at a particular moment. . . .

If this sounds incoherent, a good part of the strength of post-democracy lies in its incoherence. By disguising what and how political decisions are made, it renders them unstoppable and perhaps irreversible. As noted above, global governance provides no serious democratic means for the "governed" to repeal decisions that they may find repellent, but that their new "governors" have, nevertheless, imposed upon them without their consent.

Another strength is that post-democracy has support from elites of the Right as well as the Left. It should not surprise us that the transnational project has been rhetorically (and sometimes financially) embraced by many multinational American-based corporations. It is perhaps understandable that transnational corporations should seek to emphasize that they are global rather than national entities. Yet it was also rather unseemly for the corporate counsel of Motorola to denounce as "nationalistic" [consumer advocate] Ralph Nader's suggestion that American-based corporations begin their stockholder meetings with "The Pledge of Allegiance" to the "country that bred them" and "defended them."

---

*In this new system, the United States . . . would cease to be an independent democratic nation, in the sense that it is today.*

---

Likewise, it was unseemly when the late Carl Gerstacker, chairman and CEO of Dow, wrote several decades ago that he dreamed of establishing the world headquarters of this American chemical giant on the "truly neutral ground" of an island "beholden to no nation or society." Of course, Dow, Motorola and a host of other corporations, whose executives have made foolish comments about their company's relationship to

America, are, indeed, "beholden" to the American nation. Without American sovereignty, mores, culture, laws and military power, they would be neither prosperous nor protected. . . .

If present patterns of discourse continue, in the end, the transnational regime would claim to be the ultimate fulfillment of democracy. Democracy, it would be explained, has simply "evolved", like "human rights" and the "new international law." It no longer means what it used to mean—majority rule with limited government based on equality of citizenship within a nation-state—in much the same way that "civil rights" no longer means equality of opportunity for individuals but rather "substantive" equality of condition for groups. Outward forms and symbols of 20th-century liberal democracy would be maintained . . . even though they had lost their substantive meaning. And no doubt a weakened and hollowed out shell of a nation-state would still exist. . . .

One of the more clever arguments for transnationalism revolves around the concept of the American nation-state leading the world to its transnational future. Of course, in achieving this goal, the American democratic regime slowly metamorphizes into a different type of entity. . . . In the end, American "leadership" comes from "following" the "international community", i.e., the worldview of transnational progressive elites. . . .

In this new system, the United States would become the key actor, the primary engine of a different type of regime, but hemmed in on all sides by constraints to its democratic sovereignty. Gradually, after decades, . . . it would cease to be an independent democratic nation, in the sense that it is today. Thus, "America" would become in reality Post-America, the core of a new post-democratic system of global governance. The "international community" would dictate policy on issues such as national defense, the Middle East, and the like, to liberal democratic nation-states. America . . . would have betrayed the great principle of self-government (consent) upon which (along with natural rights) our nation was founded.

# The Spread of Global Free-Market Democracy Causes Ethnic Violence

*Amy Chua*

**About the author**: *Amy Chua is a professor at Yale Law School. She lectures frequently on the effects of globalization to government, business, and academic groups.*

The prevailing view among globalization's supporters is that markets and democracy are a kind of universal prescription for the multiple ills of underdevelopment. Market capitalism is the most efficient economic system the world has ever known. Democracy is the fairest political system the world has ever known and the one most respectful of individual liberty. Working hand in hand, markets and democracy will gradually transform the world into a community of prosperous, war-shunning nations, and individuals into liberal, civic-minded citizens and consumers. In the process, ethnic hatred, religious zealotry, and other "backward" aspects of underdevelopment will be swept away. . . .

For globalization's enthusiasts, the cure for group hatred and ethnic violence around the world is straightforward: more markets and more democracy. Thus after the September 11 attacks, [*New York Times* columnist Thomas] Friedman published an op-ed piece pointing to India and Bangladesh as good "role models" for the Middle East and arguing that the solution to terrorism and militant Islam is: "Hello? Hello? There's a message here. It's democracy, stupid!"—"[m]ulti-ethnic, pluralistic, free-market democracy."

Amy Chua, *World on Fire*. New York: Random House, 2003, pp. 7–13.

## Globalization and Ethnic Violence

By contrast, . . . [my thesis] is that the global spread of markets and democracy is a principal, aggravating cause of group hatred and ethnic violence throughout the non-Western world. In the numerous societies around the world that have a market-dominant minority, markets and democracy are not mutually reinforcing. Because markets and democracy benefit different ethnic groups in such societies, the pursuit of free market democracy produces highly unstable and combustible conditions. Markets concentrate enormous wealth in the hands of an "outsider" minority, fomenting ethnic envy and hatred among often chronically poor majorities. In absolute terms the majority may or may not be better off—a dispute that much of the globalization debate fixates on—but any sense of improvement is overwhelmed by their continuing poverty and the hated minority's extraordinary economic success. More humiliating still, market-dominant minorities, along with their foreign-investor partners, invariably come to control the crown jewels of the economy, often symbolic of the nation's patrimony and identity—oil in Russia and Venezuela, diamonds in South Africa, silver and tin in Bolivia, jade, teak, and rubies in Burma.

---

*When free market democracy is pursued in the presence of a market-dominant minority, the almost invariable result is backlash.*

---

Introducing democracy in these circumstances does not transform voters into open-minded cocitizens in a national community. Rather, the competition for votes fosters the emergence of demagogues who scapegoat the resented minority and foment active ethnonationalist movements demanding that the country's wealth and identity be reclaimed by the "true owners of the nation." As America celebrated the global spread of democracy in the 1990s, ethnicized political slogans proliferated: "Georgia for the Georgians," "Eritreans Out of Ethiopia," "Kenya for Kenyans," "Venezuela for *Pardos*," "Kazakhstan for Kazakhs," "Serbia for Serbs," "Croatia for Croats," "Hutu Power," "Assam for Assamese," "Jews Out of Russia." . . .

## Backlash Against Globalization

When free market democracy is pursued in the presence of a market-dominant minority, the almost invariable result is backlash. This backlash typically takes one of three forms. The first is a backlash against markets, targeting the market-dominant minority's wealth. The second is a backlash against democracy by forces favorable to the market-dominant minority. The third is violence, sometimes genocidal, directed against the market-dominant minority itself.

Zimbabwe today is a vivid illustration of the first kind of backlash—an ethnically targeted anti-market backlash. For several years now President Robert Mugabe has encouraged the violent seizure of 10 million acres of white-owned commercial farmland. As one Zimbabwean explained, "The land belongs to us. The foreigners should not own land here. There is no black Zimbabwean who owns land in England. Why should any European own land here?" Mugabe himself was more explicit: "Strike fear in the heart of the white man, our real enemy!" Most of the country's white "foreigners" are third-generation Zimbabweans. Just 1 percent of the population, they have for generations controlled 70 percent of the country's best land, largely in the form of highly productive three-thousand-acre tobacco and sugar farms.

Watching Zimbabwe's economy take a free fall as a result of the mass landgrab, the United States and United Kingdom together with dozens of human rights groups urged President Mugabe to step down, calling resoundingly for "free and fair elections." But the idea that *democracy* is the answer to Zimbabwe's problems is breathtakingly naive. Perhaps Mugabe would have lost the 2002 elections in the absence of foul play.

Even if so, it is important to remember that Mugabe himself is a product of democracy. The hero of Zimbabwe's black liberation movement and a master manipulator of masses, he swept to victory in the closely monitored elections of 1980, promising to expropriate "stolen" white land. Repeating that promise has helped him win every election since. Moreover, Mugabe's land-seizure campaign was another product of the democratic process. It was deftly timed in anticipation of the 2000 and 2002 elections, and deliberately calculated to mobilize popular support for Mugabe's teetering regime.

In the contest between an economically powerful ethnic minority and a numerically powerful impoverished majority, the majority does not always prevail. Instead of a backlash against the market, another likely outcome is a backlash against democracy, favoring the market-dominant minority at the expense of majority will. Examples of this dynamic are extremely common. Indeed, . . . the world's most notorious cases of "crony capitalism" all involve a market-dominant ethnic minority—from Ferdinand Marcos's Chinese-protective dictatorship in the Philippines to President Siaka Stevens's shadow alliance with five Lebanese diamond dealers in Sierra Leone to President Daniel Arap Moi's "business arrangements" with a handful of Indian tycoons in Kenya today.

*Western critics of globalization have overlooked the ethnic dimensions of market disparities.*

The third and most ferocious kind of backlash is majority-supported violence aimed at eliminating a market-dominant minority. Two recent examples are the ethnic cleansing of Croats in the former Yugoslavia and the mass slaughter of Tutsi in Rwanda. In both cases a resented and disproportionately prosperous ethnic minority was attacked by members of a relatively impoverished majority, incited by an ethnonationalist government. In other words, markets and democracy were among the causes of both the Rwandan and Yugoslavian genocides. . . .

## Globalization's Critics Misguided

To their credit, critics of globalization have called attention to the grotesque imbalances that free markets produce. In the 1990s, writes Thomas Frank in *One Market under God*, global markets made "the corporation the most powerful institution on earth," transformed "CEOs as a class into one of the wealthiest elites of all time," and, from America to Indonesia, "forgot about the poor with a decisiveness we hadn't seen since the 1920s." Joining Frank in his criticism of "the almighty market" is a host of strange bedfellows: American farmers and factory workers opposed to NAFTA [North American Free Trade Agreement], environmentalists, the AFL-CIO, human rights activists, Third World [developing countries] advocates, and sundry other groups that made up the protesters at Seattle, Davos, Genoa, and New York City. Defenders of globalization respond, with some justification, that the world's poor would be even worse off without global marketization. With some important exceptions, including most of Africa, recent World Bank studies show that globalization's "trickle down" has produced benefits for the poor as well as the rich in developing countries.

More fundamentally, however, like their pro-globalization counterparts, Western critics of globalization have overlooked the ethnic dimension of market disparities. They tend to see wealth and poverty in terms of class conflict, not ethnic conflict. This perspective might make sense in the advanced Western societies, but the ethnic realities of the developing world are completely different from those of the West. As a result, the solutions that globalization's critics propose are often shortsighted and even dangerous when applied to non-Western societies.

Essentially, the anti-globalization movement asks for one thing: more democracy. Thus [scholar and political activist] Noam Chomsky, one of the movement's high priests, has clarified that there is no struggle against "globalization" in the general sense, only a struggle against the global "neoliberalism" perpetuated by a few "masters of the universe" at the expense of a truly democratic community. Similarly, at the 2002 World Social Forum in Brazil, Lori Wallach of Public Citizen [a consumer advocacy organization] rejected the label "anti-globalization," explaining that "our movement, really, is globally for democracy, equality, diversity, justice and quality of life." Wallach has also warned that the WTO [World Trade Organization] must "either bend to the will of the people worldwide or it will break." Echoing these voices are literally dozens of NGOs [nongovernmental organization] who call for "democratically empowering the poor majorities of the world."

---

*Just as it is dangerous to view markets as the panacea for the world's poverty and strife, so too it is dangerous to see democracy as a panacea.*

---

Given the ethnic dynamics of the developing world, and in particular the phenomenon of market-dominant minorities, merely "empowering the poor majorities of the world" is not enough. Empowering the Hutu majority in Rwanda did not produce desirable consequences. Nor did empowering the Serbian majority in Serbia.

Critics of globalization are right to demand that more attention be paid to the enormous wealth disparities created by global markets. But just as it is dangerous to view markets as the panacea for the world's poverty and strife, so too it is dangerous to see democracy as a panacea. Markets and democracy may well offer the best long-run economic and political hope for developing and post-Communist societies. In the short run, however, they are part of the problem.

# Globalization Promotes Democracy Both Directly and Indirectly

*Jagdish Bhagwati*

**About the author**: *Jagdish Bhagwati is a professor of economics and law at Columbia University in New York, an advisor to the United Nations and the World Trade Organization, and a senior fellow for international economics at the Council on Foreign Relations, a nonpartisan think-tank for foreign policy issues. Bhagwati is the author of the book,* In Defense of Globalization *(2004), from which the following viewpoint is excerpted.*

Globalization promotes democracy both directly and indirectly. The direct link comes from the fact that rural farmers are now able to bypass the dominant classes and castes by taking their produce directly to the market thanks to modern information technology, thereby loosening the control of these traditionally hegemonic groups. In turn, this can start them on the way to becoming more-independent actors, with democratic aspirations, in the political arena.

Globalization is at the source of this phenomenon in two ways: the computers themselves are available because of trade, and the markets accessed are foreign in many cases, not just domestic. Thus, a recent report from Kamalpur village in India by the *Wall Street Journal* reporter Cris Prystay documents how the villagers are now selling their crops by computer, cutting out the middlemen.

> Soybean farmer Mohammed Arif, 24 years old, says the computer allows farmers greater control over their own goods. Farmers often get cheated at markets, or get stuck with whatever price is offered that day. With the computer, he says, they can make a considered decision at home, holding crops until prices improve.

Jagdish Bhagwati, *In Defense of Globalization.* New York: Oxford University Press, 2004, pp. 92–105.

## The Link Between Prosperity and Democracy

The indirect link, on the other hand, comes from a proposition vigorously advanced by the American political scientist and intellectual Seymour Martin Lipset in his 1959 classic *Some Social Requisites of Democracy*. . . .

The thesis popularly attributed to Lipset has . . . been that economic prosperity produces a middle class. This emerging middle class creates, however haltingly, an effective demand for democratization of politics: the new bourgeoisie, with wallets a little fatter, seeks a political voice, not just one in the marketplace.

So, as with the thesis successfully linking globalization with reduced poverty, we now have another two-step argument: globalization leads to prosperity, and prosperity in turn leads to democratization of politics with the rise of the middle class. The first step is supported by evidence. Is the second step also?

There is no doubt that many believe it to be true. Indeed, many politicians embrace it passionately. In arguing for China's entry into the World Trade Organization, Congressman Tom DeLay confidently asserted, "Entrepreneurs, once condemned as 'counter-revolutionaries', are now the instruments of reform. . . . [T]his middle class will eventually demand broad acceptance of democratic values." President Bill Clinton, also supporting China's entry, argued that "as China's people become more mobile, prosperous, and aware of alternative ways of life, they will seek greater say in the decisions that affect their lives." President George W. Bush has also spoken in the same vein: "It is important for us to trade with China to encourage the growth of an entrepreneurial class [because when we do this] you'll be amazed at how soon democracy will come."

The strong belief that economic prosperity, engineered through globalization as also the fostering of economic freedoms and associated use of markets rather than central planning, will promote democracy has also been at the heart of a different impassioned debate, contrasting the Russian and the Chinese experience. Russia under Gorbachev opted for glasnost (political freedom and democracy) before perestroika (economic restructuring);. . . China opted for economic change while keeping democratization firmly away. China's enormous success and Russia's astonishing failure have led many to think both that democratization should follow, not precede, economic reforms, and that, as Lipset would have it, the prosperity and the middle classes that follow the success of economic reforms will indeed lead to democratization down the road. . . .

After the massive shift to democracy that began in the 1980s, the thesis received a new lease on life. As the political scientist Sheri Berman has stated: "Wherever one looked—from Southern Europe to East Asia, from Latin America to the Soviet Union—it seemed as if transitions were the order of the day. In many cases, furthermore, the transitions seemed to follow impressive periods of economic development or correlate with a shift to a free-market economy." And it is noteworthy that, after reviewing three decades of literature on the link between economic development and democracy, the political scientist Larry Diamond concluded that the evidence broadly supported Lipset's proposed link between development and the rise of democracy.

## The Role of the Middle Class

But if the link between development and the rise of democracy is robust, Lipset's causation in the shape of the rise and role of the middle class is less so. There is, of course, some evidence in favor of this explanation. Middle classes, particularly today, have greater contacts with other societies by travel, video, radio, and television and hence indulge in more seditious thoughts and a diverse range of protests that include samizdat. [Political scientists] Juan Linz and Alfred Stepan note that there is "even strong empirical evidence that increases in regional wealth increase citizens' expectations that they should be well treated by the police."

---

*The Internet, despite attempts at regulating it, is working its insidious way into . . . [China's Communist Party] system.*

---

Yet factors other than the rise of the middle class have played a role. Thus Linz and Stepan make the fascinating observation—based on Pinochet's regime in Chile, Brazil in the early 1970s, and two decades in Franco's Spain—that while there was willingness to put up with authoritarian regimes as long as they were delivering development, this willingness disappeared once development was delivered and prosperity seemed to be securely in place. . . .

It is also well to remember some notable recent experiences that do not really support the role-of-the-middle-class thesis. Consider the way democracy was ushered into Indonesia and South Korea in the immediate aftermath of the Asian financial crisis in 1997–98. Democracy came not as a result of orderly, gentle opening of the door as bourgeois groups increased with economic prosperity and demanded more political rights. It was instead a result of the economic upheaval that the crisis wreaked: the authoritarian elites were discredited and swept away! The mismanagement of globalization and its malign impact were what really produced the swift transition to democracy.

Then again, the benign China scenario—that rapid development will democratize China—has also been challenged, but the criticisms are frankly not persuasive. . . . The political oversight of the Communist Party over the society and the polity are evident to all who see without wearing blinkers. Yet local elections have taken place. The Internet, despite attempts at regulating it, is working its insidious way into the system. Trade and investment, though concentrated in the four dynamic coastal provinces, are creating new consumers, new producers, and new links with the outside world and its capitalist allures and democratic ways. To assert that all this will not nudge, even push, the communist regime into more political freedoms seems to be to confuse inertia with rigor mortis.

# Global Economic Development Is a Tool for Encouraging Democracy

*Daniel T. Griswold*

**About the author**: *Daniel T. Griswold is the director of the Center for Trade Policy Studies, part of the Cato Institute, a public, non-profit policy research organization that advocates libertarian principles of limited government, individual liberty, free markets, and peace.*

In the aftermath of September 11 [2001], the foreign policy dimension of trade has reasserted itself. Expanding trade, especially with and among less developed countries, is once again being recognized as a tool for encouraging democracy and respect for human rights in regions and countries of the world where those commodities have been the exception rather than the rule. . . .

## How Free Markets Foster Political Freedoms

Economic openness and the commercial competition and contact it brings can directly and indirectly promote civil and political freedoms within countries. Trade can influence the political system directly by increasing the contact a nation's citizens experience with the rest of the world, through face-to-face meetings, and electronic communications, including telephone, fax, and the Internet. Commercial communication can bring a sharing of ideas and exposure to new ways of thinking, doing business, and organizing civil society. Along with the flow of consumer and industrial goods often come books, magazines, and other media with political and social content. Foreign investment and services trade create opportunities for

Daniel T. Griswold, "Trading Tyranny for Freedom," Cato Institute, Center for Trade Policy Studies, January 6, 2004. www.freetrade.org/pubs/pas/tpa-026.pdf.

foreign travel and study, allowing citizens to experience first-hand the civil liberties and more representative political institutions of other nations.

Economic freedom and trade provide a counterweight to governmental power. A free market diffuses economic decisionmaking among millions of producers and consumers rather than leaving it in the hands of a few centralized government actors who could, and often do, use that power to suppress or marginalize political opposition. . . .

---

*Economic development raises expectations that change and progress are possible.*

---

This dispersion of economic control, in turn, creates space for nongovernmental organizations and private-sector alternatives to political leadership—in short, civil society. A thriving private economy creates sources of funding for nonstate institutions, which in turn can provide ideas, influence, and leadership outside the existing government. A more pluralistic social and political culture greatly enhances the prospects for a more pluralistic and representative political system. Private-sector corporations, both domestic and foreign-owned, create an alternate source of wealth, influence, and leadership. . . .

Just as important, economic freedom and openness encourage democracy indirectly by raising living standards and expanding the middle class. Economic theory and evidence lean heavily toward the conclusion that open economies tend to grow faster and achieve higher incomes than closed economies. The *Economic Freedom of the World* study by James Gwartney and Robert Lawson found that nations that ranked in the top quintile in terms of economic openness from 1980 to 1998 experienced annual economic growth that was almost five times faster (2.4 percent vs. 0.5 percent) than those nations in the bottom quintile of openness. People living in the most open economies enjoyed far higher annual incomes per capita ($22,306 vs. $2,916) than those living in the most closed economies. A study by World Bank economists David Dollar and Aart Kraay found that less developed countries that opened themselves to the global economy grew much faster than those that remained relatively closed. Other academic studies have reached similar conclusions.

The faster growth and greater wealth that accompany trade promote democracy by creating an economically independent and politically aware middle class. A sizeable or dominant middle class means that more citizens can afford to be educated and take an interest in public affairs. As citizens acquire assets and establish business and careers in the private sector, they prefer the continuity and evolutionary reform of a democratic system to the sharp turns and occasional revolutions of more authoritarian systems. People who are allowed to successfully manage their daily economic lives in a relatively free market come to expect and demand more freedom in the political and social realms.

---

*Thirty years ago democracies were the exception in Latin America, while today they are the rule.*

---

Economic development raises expectations that change and progress are possible. In less developed countries, it often leads to growing urbanization, which fosters greater literacy, communication, and access to alternative media. Palpable material progress can take the steam out of radical political movements that feed on frustration and hopelessness, and increase tolerance for minority ethnic and political groups. Ruling elites tend to treat their middle-class countrymen with more respect and deference than they would those in the impoverished and uneducated lower classes. . . .

Wealth by itself does not promote democracy if the wealth is controlled by the state or a small ruling elite. A resource-rich country can have a relatively high per capita gross domestic product, but if its natural wealth is centrally held and does not nurture an autonomous middle class that earns its wealth independently of the state, the prospects for political pluralism, civil liberties, and democracy are probably no better than in a poor country without resources. For wealth to cultivate the soil for democracy, it must be produced, retained, and controlled by a broad base of society, and for wealth to be created in that manner, an economy must be relatively open and free.

## Reality Reflects Free Market Theory

The reality of the world today broadly reflects those theoretical links between trade, free markets, and political and civil freedom. As trade and globalization have spread to more and more countries in the last 30 years, so too have democracy and political and civil freedoms. In particular, people who live in countries that are relatively open to trade are much more likely to live in democracies and enjoy full civil and political freedoms than those who live in countries relatively closed to trade. Nations that have followed a path of trade reform in recent decades by progressively opening themselves to the global economy are significantly more likely to have expanded their citizens' political and civil freedoms.

The recent trend toward globalization has been accompanied by a trend toward greater political and civil liberty around the world. In the past 30 years, cross-border flows of trade, investment, and currency have increased dramatically, and far faster than output itself. Trade barriers have fallen unilaterally and through multilateral and regional trade agreements in Latin America; the former Soviet bloc nations; East Asia, including China; and more developed nations as well.

During that same period, political and civil liberties have been spreading around the world. Thirty years ago democracies were the exception in Latin America, while today they are the rule. Many former communist states from the old Soviet

Union and its empire have successfully transformed themselves into functioning democracies that protect basic civil and political freedoms. In East Asia, democracy and respect for human rights have replaced authoritarian rule in South Korea, Taiwan, Thailand, the Philippines, and Indonesia.

According to Freedom House, a New York-based human rights organization, the share of the world's population that enjoys full civil and political liberties has risen sharply in the past three decades. The share of the world's people who live in countries Freedom House classifies as "Free"—meaning "countries in which there is broad scope for open political competition, a climate of respect for civil liberties, significant independent civic life, and independent media"—has jumped from 35 percent in 1973 to 44 percent today. Meanwhile, the share of people living in countries classified as "Not Free"—"where basic political rights are absent and basic civil liberties were widely and systematically denied"—has dropped from 47 to 35 percent. . . .

## The United States Should Promote Freer Trade and Democracy

Theory and evidence together argue that trade liberalization and a more general openness to the global economy do correlate with more political and civil freedom, in the world as a whole and within individual countries. . . .

By opening our markets at home and encouraging freer trade abroad, the United States promotes not only economic growth but a more humane and democratic world. Free trade and globalization do not guarantee democracy and respect for human rights, but they do provide a more favorable trade wind for achieving those goals. Members of Congress who consistently vote against more open markets at home and market-opening trade agreements with other nations are in effect voting to keep millions of people locked within the walls of tyranny, and millions more trapped in a partly free netherworld of half-rights, half-freedoms, and half-democracy.

In light of the evidence that free trade promotes democracy and civil freedoms, policy-makers in Washington need to ask themselves: How can we fully ensure our security as a nation when billions of people around the world are denied their most basic rights to civil freedom, representative government, and the opportunity to realize their productive potential in the marketplace? And how can we encourage the spread of democracy and human rights if billions of people remain trapped in poverty and economic stagnation, lacking freedom, education, and the most basic tools of modern life? And how can we hope to see them escape that poverty to join the independent middle class without allowing them to participate in the global marketplace?

Human liberties cannot be neatly compartmentalized. Expanding the freedom of people to engage in transactions across international borders over time enlarges their freedom to exercise autonomy over other, noncommercial aspects of their daily lives and to shape and choose a government that will protect those basic rights. If it is in our national interest to encourage the expansion of human rights and democracy abroad—and it most certainly is—the U.S. government should also champion the expansion of international trade and commerce.

# The Nation-State Will Survive Globalization

## Martin Wolf

**About the author**: *Martin Wolf is an associate editor and the chief economics commentator at the* Financial Times, *a newspaper based in the United Kingdom that covers international business and finance matters.*

A specter is haunting the world's governments—the specter of globalization. Some argue that predatory market forces make it impossible for benevolent governments to shield their populations from the beasts of prey that lurk beyond their borders. Others counter that benign market forces actually prevent predatory governments from fleecing their citizens. Although the two sides see different villains, they draw one common conclusion: omnipotent markets mean impotent politicians. Indeed, this formula has become one of the cliches of our age. But is it true that governments have become weaker and less relevant than ever before? And does globalization, by definition, have to be the nemesis of national government?. . .

## Tradeoffs Facing States

Economies are . . . never entirely open or entirely closed. Opening requires governments to loosen three types of economic controls: on capital flows, goods and services, and people. Liberalizing one of the above neither requires nor always leads to liberalization in the others. Free movement of goods and services makes regulating capital flows more difficult, but not impossible; foreign direct investment can flow across national barriers to trade in goods without knocking them down. It is easier still to trade freely and abolish controls on capital movement, while nevertheless regulating movement of people.

Martin Wolf, "Will the Nation-State Survive Globalization?" *Foreign Affairs*, January–February 2001, vol. 80, iss. 1, p. 178.

The important questions, then, concern the tradeoffs confronting governments that have chosen a degree of international economic integration. How constrained will governments find themselves once they have chosen openness?. . .

## Constraints on Taxes

Globalization is often perceived as destroying governments' capacities to do what they want or need, particularly in the key areas of taxation, public spending for income redistribution, and macroeconomic policy. But how true is this perception?

In fact, no evidence supports the conclusion that states can no longer raise taxes. On the contrary: in 1999, EU [European Union] governments spent or redistributed an average of 47 percent of their GDPs [gross domestic product]. An important new book by Vito Tanzi of the IMF [International Monetary Fund] and Ludger Schuknecht at the European Central Bank underlines this point. Over the course of the twentieth century, the average share of government spending among Organization for Economic Cooperation and Development (OECD) member states jumped from an eighth to almost half of GDP. In some high-income countries such as France and Germany, these ratios were higher than ever before.

Until now, it has been electoral resistance, not globalization, that has most significantly limited the growth in taxation. Tanzi claims that this is about to change. He argues that collecting taxes is becoming harder due to a long list of "fiscal termites" gnawing at the foundations of taxation regimes: more cross-border shopping, the increased mobility of skilled labor, the growth of electronic commerce, the expansion of tax havens, the development of new financial instruments and intermediaries, growing trade within multinational companies, and the possible replacement of bank accounts with electronic money embedded in "smart cards." . . . This sense of threat has grown out of several fiscal developments produced by globalization: increased mobility of people and money, greater difficulty in collecting information on income and spending, and the impact of the Internet on information flows and collection.

---

*[One] aspect of globalization, the Internet, may have an appreciable impact on tax collection.*

---

Yet the competitive threat that governments face must not be exaggerated. The fiscal implications of labor, capital, and spending mobility are already evident in local jurisdictions that have the freedom to set their own tax rates. Even local governments can impose higher taxes than their neighbors, provided they contain specific resources or offer location-specific amenities that residents desire and consume. . . . Eliminating legal barriers to mobility therefore constrains, but does not eliminate, the ability of some jurisdictions to levy far higher taxes than others. . . .

The international mobility of people and goods is unlikely ever to come close to the kind of mobility that exists between states in the United States. Legal, linguistic, and cultural barriers will keep levels of cross-border migration far lower than levels of movement within any given country. Since taxes on labor income and spending are the predominant source of national revenue, the modern country's income base seems quite safe. . . .

[One] aspect of globalization, the Internet, may have an appreciable impact on tax collection. Stephane Buydens of the OECD plausibly argues that the Internet will primarily affect four main areas: taxes on spending, tax treaties, internal pricing of multinational companies, and tax administration. Purely Internet-based transactions—downloading of films, software, or music—are hard to tax. But when the Internet is used to buy tangible goods, governments can impose taxes, provided that the suppliers cooperate with the fiscal authorities of their corresponding jurisdictions. To the extent that these suppliers are large shareholder-owned companies, which they usually are, this cooperation may not be as hard to obtain as is often supposed. . . .

The overall conclusion, then, is that economic liberalization and technology advances will make taxation significantly more challenging. . . . The bottom line is that the opening of economies and the blossoming of new technologies are reinforcing constraints that have already developed within domestic politics. National governments are becoming a little more like local governments. . . .

## Constraints on Social Spending and Fiscal Policy

Meanwhile, governments can continue the practice of income redistribution to the extent that the most highly taxed citizens and firms cannot—or do not wish to—evade taxation. In fact, if taxes are used to fund what are believed to be location-specific benefits, such as income redistribution or welfare spending, taxpayers will likely be quite willing to pay, perhaps because they either identify with the beneficiaries, fear that they could become indigent themselves, or treasure the security that comes from living among people who are not destitute. Taxpayers may also feel a sense of moral obligation to the poor, a sentiment that seems stronger in small, homogeneous societies. Alternatively, they may merely be unable to evade or avoid those taxes without relocating physically outside the jurisdiction. For all these reasons, sustaining a high measure of redistributive taxation remains perfectly possible. The constraint is not globalization, but the willingness of the electorate to tolerate high taxation.

Last but not least, some observers argue that globalization limits governments' ability to run fiscal deficits and pursue inflationary monetary policy. But macroeconomic policy is always vulnerable to the reaction of the private sector, regardless of whether the capital market is internationally integrated. If a government pursues a consistently inflationary policy, long-term nominal interest rates will rise, partly to compensate for inflation and partly to insure the bondholders against inflation risk. Similarly, if a government relies on the printing press to finance its activity, a flight from money into goods, services, and assets will ensue—and, in turn, generate inflation.

---

*A country that chooses international economic integration implicitly accepts constraints on its actions.*

---

Within one country, these reactions may be slow. A government can pursue an inflationary policy over a long period and boost the economy; the price may not have to be paid for many years. What difference, then, does it make for the country to be open to international capital flows? The most important change is that the reaction of a government's creditors is likely to be quicker and more brutal because they have more alternatives. This response will often show itself in a collapsing exchange rate, as happened in East Asia in 1997 and 1998.

## The Continuing Importance of States

A country that chooses international economic integration implicitly accepts constraints on its actions. Nevertheless, the idea that these constraints wither away the state's capacity to tax, regulate, or intervene is wrong. Rather, international economic integration accelerates the market's responses to policy by increasing the range of alternative options available to those affected. There are also powerful reasons for believing that the constraints imposed on (or voluntarily accepted by) governments by globalization are, on balance, desirable.

For example, the assumption that most governments are benevolent welfare-maximizers is naive. International economic integration creates competition among governments—even countries that fiercely resist integration cannot survive with uncompetitive economies, as shown by the fate of the Soviet Union. This competition constrains the ability of governments to act in a predatory manner and increases the incentive to provide services that are valued by those who pay the bulk of the taxes.

Another reason for welcoming the constraints is that self-imposed limits on a government's future actions enhance the credibility of even a benevolent government's commitments to the private sector. An open capital account is one such constraint. Treaties with other governments, as in the WTO [World Trade Organization], are another, as are agreements with powerful private parties. Even China has come to recognize the economic benefits that it can gain from international commitments of this kind.

The proposition that globalization makes states unnecessary is even less credible than the idea that it makes states impotent. If anything, the exact opposite is true, for at least three reasons. First, the ability of a society to take advantage of the opportunities offered by international economic integration depends on the quality of public goods, such as property rights, an honest civil service, personal security, and basic education. Without an appropriate legal framework, in particular, the web of potentially rewarding contracts is vastly reduced. This point may seem trivial, but many developing economies have failed to achieve these essential preconditions of success.

Second, the state normally defines identity. A sense of belonging is part of the people's sense of security, and one that most people would not want to give up, even in the age of globalization. It is perhaps not surprising that some of the most successfully integrated economies are small, homogeneous countries with a strong sense of collective identity.

Third, international governance rests on the ability of individual states to provide and guarantee stability. The bedrock of international order is the territorial state with its monopoly on coercive power within its jurisdiction. Cyberspace does not change this: economies are ultimately run for and by human beings, who have a physical presence and, therefore, a physical location.

---

*As the source of order and basis of governance, the state will remain in the future as effective . . . as it has ever been.*

---

Globalization does not make states unnecessary. On the contrary, for people to be successful in exploiting the opportunities afforded by international integration, they need states at both ends of their transactions. Failed states, disorderly states, weak states, and corrupt states are shunned as the black holes of the global economic system.

What, then, does globalization mean for states? First, policy ultimately determines the pace and depth of international economic integration. For each country, globalization is at least as much a choice as a destiny. Second, in important respects—notably a country's monetary regime, capital account, and above all, labor mobility—the policy underpinnings of integration are less complete than they were a century ago. Third, countries choose integration because they see its benefits. Once chosen, any specific degree of international integration imposes constraints on the ability of governments to tax, redistribute income, and influence macroeconomic conditions. But those constraints must not be exaggerated, and their effects are often beneficial. Fourth, international economic integration magnifies the impact of the difference between good and bad states—between states that provide public goods and those that serve predatory private interests, including those of the rulers.

Finally, as the world economy continues to integrate and cross-border flows become more important, global governance must be improved. Global governance will come not at the expense of the state but rather as an expression of the interests that the state embodies. As the source of order and basis of governance, the state will remain in the future as effective, and will be as essential, as it has ever been.

# Glossary

**Capitalism** A concept that describes the economic system of the United States, European countries, and other industrialized nations, in which businesses and the means of production are privately owned and operated for profit.

**Central America Free Trade Agreement (CAFTA)** An agreement signed on May 28, 2004 to expand NAFTA to five Central American nations (Guatemala, El Salvador, Honduras, Costa Rica and Nicaragua), and the Dominican Republic.

**Developing (or Underdeveloped) Countries** A term often used to describe countries that have not yet industrialized or have not developed their economies to the level of nations such as the United States and those in Europe.

**Economic Liberalization** A term that refers to the relaxation of previous government restrictions on trade.

**Fair Trade** A term used to describe an alternative trade system in which smaller, less-developed countries would have a greater say in trade matters and in which issues such as poverty, the environment, workers' rights, and other social issues are given more weight than in current trade relationships.

**Foreign Direct Investment** The purchase or construction of tangible assets, such as land, factories, machines, buildings, and businesses in one country by individuals or businesses located in another country.

**Free Trade** A term that refers to trade agreements between countries in which tariffs and other barriers to the free flow of goods and services are eliminated.

**Free Trade Area of the Americas (FTAA)** A proposed agreement to eliminate or reduce trade barriers among all countries in the Western Hemisphere except Cuba.

**G8 or Group of 8** A group of eight leaders from the most economically and politically powerful countries of the world, including the United States, Canada, Britain, Germany, Japan, Italy, France, and Russia.

**General Agreement on Trade and Tariffs (GATT)** An agreement negotiated in 1947 among 23 countries to increase international trade by reducing tariffs and other trade barriers, providing rules for international commerce, and creating a framework for periodic multilateral negotiations on trade issues.

**Globalization** A term that generally refers to the increasing interconnectedness and interdependence between nations, especially in the area of global trade, caused largely by recent technological advances in communications and transportation that make it easier for people to travel, communicate, and do business internationally.

**International Monetary Fund (IMF)** An international organization set up in 1944 to lower trade barriers and stabilize currency exchange rates between nations.

**Multinational Corporation (MNC)** A business operating in many countries, with a headquarters and business structure in each country. Two-thirds of the world's trade takes place between multinational corporations and their subsidiary corporations and branches.

**Neoliberalism** The philosophy behind economic globalization, which includes beliefs in free markets, minimum barriers to the flow of goods, services, and capital, and conditions that free business from interference by government.

**Nongovernmental Organizations (NGOs)** Private groups, organized on a local, national, or international level, that advocate for particular causes, such as helping the poor, protecting the environment, providing social services, or undertaking community development.

**North American Free Trade Agreement (NAFTA)** A trade agreement between the United States, Canada, and Mexico, which took effect January 1, 1994, and is designed to promote freer trade between the three nations.

**Organization for Economic Cooperation and Development (OECD)** An organization of thirty member countries committed to democratic government, market economies, and the promotion of free trade.

**Sustainable Development** Economic development that meets the needs of the present without compromising the ability of future generations to meet their own needs, with a focus on areas such as poverty, health, and the environment.

**Transnational Corporation (TNC)** A business that has its headquarters in one country with manufacturing or other operations and branches in many different countries. Monsanto and Sony Corporation are examples of TNCs.

**World Bank** An international institution set up in 1944 to help rebuild Europe after World War II, which today focuses on bringing "underdeveloped" nations into the international economy.

**World Trade Organization (WTO)** An international organization of 144 member countries that encourages global trade between member nations, administers global trade agreements, and resolves disputes between member countries about trade issues.

# Chronology

### July 1944

The world's leading economists, politicians, bankers, and corporate leaders meet at Bretton Woods, New Hampshire, to decide how to respond to the devastation of World War II. Agreements are signed that create the World Bank and the International Monetary Fund (IMF). Both institutions are designed to provide economic assistance to war-damaged countries.

### June 1945

The United Nations is established.

### October 1947

In Geneva, Switzerland, twenty-three countries sign the General Agreement on Tariffs and Trade (GATT), a treaty to promote free global trade.

### 1948

GATT goes into force.

### 1949

The World Bank and the IMF begin operations. They offer loans to undeveloped governments to assist them in developing their economies similar to those of industrialized nations. Second round of GATT trade talks is held at Annecy, France, and countries agree to more than 5,000 trade concessions.

### 1950

Third round of GATT talks is held in Torquay, England, where countries exchanged some 8,700 tariff concessions.

## 1955–1956

The next GATT trade talks are completed in May 1956, resulting in $2.5 billion in tariff reductions.

## 1960–1962

Fifth round of GATT talks yields trade concessions worth $4.9 billion, discussion about the creation of the European Economic Community.

## 1964–1967

Sixth round of GATT talks achieves tariff cuts worth $40 billion.

## 1972

The United States ends the gold standard, allowing banks and corporations to move money to and from worldwide operations with a phone call.

## 1973–1979

The seventh round of GATT talks in Tokyo, Japan, produces tariff cuts worth more than $300 billion dollars, as well as reductions in other trade barriers, such as subsidies and import licenses.

## 1980

When underdeveloped countries are unable to repay loans, the World Bank and the IMF impose austerity programs that cut wages, eliminate social welfare programs, and promote foreign investment.

## 1986–1993

GATT trade talks in Punta Del Este, Uruguay, lead to major reductions in agricultural subsidies, an agreement to allow full access for textiles and clothing from developing countries, and an extension of intellectual property rights.

**1991**

The Cold War between democracy and communism ends with the collapse of the Soviet Union.

**January 1994**

Final GATT meeting at Marrakesh, Morocco, creates the World Trade Organization (WTO), an international institution that promotes liberal global trade. GATT becomes the economic law of the world and allows corporations to challenge governmental regulations and laws that are judged to be barriers to trade. The North American Free Trade Agreement (NAFTA) goes into effect, providing for free trade between Mexico, the United States, and Canada.

**1995**

The World Trade Organization is established in Geneva.

**July 1997**

The Asian financial crisis begins and leads to bankruptcy in South Korea, Indonesia, and Thailand.

**1999**

The Secretary-General of the UN proposes a "Global Compact" at the World Economic Forum meeting in Davos, Switzerland.

**November 1999**

Large-scale public protests erupt against globalization in Seattle, Washington, disrupting WTO talks.

**April 2000**

The WTO and IMF hold annual spring meetings in Washington, D.C., and are accompanied by large-scale public protests.

### November 2001

WTO members meet in Doha, Qatar, and agree on the Doha Development Agenda, an agreement that calls for negotiations on opening markets to agricultural and manufactured goods, and services.

### December 2001

China formally joins the WTO. Taiwan is admitted weeks later.

### August 2002

The WTO rules in favor of the European Union (EU) in a dispute with the United States over tax breaks for U.S. exporters. The EU is permitted to impose $4 billion in sanctions against the United States, the highest damages ever awarded by the WTO.

### September 2002

The WTO announces an agreement designed to give developing countries access to cheap medicines, but aid agencies are disappointed with the deal.

### September 2003

World trade talks in Cancun, Mexico, collapse after four days of disagreements over farm subsidies and access to markets. Rich countries abandon plans to include issues of investment, competition policy, and public procurement in the trade talks.

### December 2003

After the WTO rules that duties imposed by the United States on imported steel are illegal, U.S. President George W. Bush repeals the tariffs to avoid a trade war with the EU.

### April 2004

The WTO rules that U.S. subsidies to its cotton farmers are unfair.

## August 2004

Trade talks in Geneva produce a framework agreement on opening up global trade. Under the agreement, the United States and the EU will reduce agricultural subsidies, while developing nations will cut tariffs on manufactured goods.

## March 2005

The WTO upholds a challenge from Brazil to U.S. subsidies to American cotton farmers.

## May 2005

The WTO agrees to start membership talks with Iran.

## October 2005

The United States offers to make big cuts in agricultural subsidies if other countries in the EU do the same.

## November 2005

The WTO approves membership for Saudi Arabia.

## December 2005

World trade talks in Hong Kong result in an agreement to conclude the round of talks begun in Doha by the end of 2006.

## July 2006

World trade talks in Geneva fail to produce agreement on lowering tariffs on agricultural goods, a step sought by less developed countries to help them fight poverty.

## July 2007

U.S. "fast track" authority, which prohibits Congress from amending trade deals negotiated by the U.S. president, is due to expire, giving the U.S. Congress much greater input into trade matters.

# Organizations to Contact

*The editors have compiled the following list of organizations concerned with the issues debated in this book. The descriptions are derived from materials provided by the organizations. All have publications or information available for interested readers. The list was compiled on the date of publication of the present volume; the information provided here may change. Be aware that many organizations take several weeks or longer to respond to inquiries, so allow as much time as possible.*

**American Enterprise Institute (AEI)**
1150 Seventeenth St. NW, Washington, DC 20036
(202) 862-5800 • fax: (202) 862-7177
Web site: www.aei.org

The American Enterprise Institute is a conservative research institute that is dedicated to preserving limited government, private enterprise, and a strong foreign policy and national defense.

**Bretton Woods Committee (BWC)**
1990 M St. NW, Suite 450, Washington, DC 20036
(202) 331-1616 • fax: (202) 785-9423
e-mail: info@brettonwoods.org
Web site: www.brettonwoods.org

BWC is a bipartisan group dedicated to increasing public understanding of international financial and development issues and the role of the World Bank, International Monetary Fund, and World Trade Organization. Members include industry and financial leaders, economists, university leaders and former government officials. On its Web site, BWC publishes the quarterly *BWC Newsletter* and reports, including *The United States and the WTO: Benefits of the Multilateral Trade System.*

## Brookings Institution
1775 Masachusetts Ave. NW, Washington, DC   20036
(202) 797-6000 • fax: (202) 797-6004
e-mail: brookinfo@brook.edu
Web site: www.brookings.org

The Brookings Institution is a think-tank that conducts research and education in the areas of foreign policy, economics, government, and the social sciences. Its Web site features numerous briefings and publications on the topic of the global economy. Examples include *The WTO and Sustainable Development, Insuring America's Workers in an Age of Offshoring,* and *Do EU Trade Policies Impoverish Developing Countries?*

## Cato Institute
1000 Massachusetts Ave. NW, Washington, DC   20036
(202) 842-0200 • fax: (202) 842-4390
e-mail: cato@cato.org
Web site: www.cato.org

The Cato Institute is a nonpartisan public policy research foundation dedicated to limiting the role of government and protecting individual liberties. It publishes the quarterly magazine *Regulation,* the bimonthly *Cato Policy Report,* and numerous policy papers and articles. Articles on globalization include *The Blessings and Challenges of Globalization, Why Globalization Works,* and *Globalization Serves the World's Poor,* which are available on its Web site.

## Competitive Enterprise Institute (CEI)
1001 Connecticut Ave. NW, Suite 1250
Washington, DC   20036
(202) 331-1010 • fax: (202) 331-0640
e-mail: info@cei.org
Web site: www.cei.org

CEI is a nonprofit public policy organization dedicated to advancing the principles of free enterprise and limited government. It believes that individuals are best helped not by government intervention, but by making their own choices in a free marketplace. CEI's publications include the monthly newsletter *Monthly Planet* and articles, including *The Winds of Global Change: Which Way Are They Blowing?* and *The Triumph Of Democratic Capitalism: The Threat of Global Governance,* which are available on its Web site.

### Earth Island Institute

300 Broadway, Suite 28, San Francisco, CA   94133
(415) 788-3666 • fax: (415) 788-7324
e-mail: earthisland@earthisland.org
Web site: www.earthisland.org

Earth Island Institute's work addresses environmental issues and their relation to such concerns as human rights and economic development in the Third World. The Institute's publications include the quarterly *Earth Island Journal.* The articles *Bucking the Corporate Future* and *In Favor of a New Protectionism* are available on its Web site.

### 50 Years Is Enough Network

3628 12th St. NE, Washington, DC   20017
(202) 463-2265
Web site: www.50years.org

Founded on the anniversary of the World Bank and International Monetary Fund, the coalitions of more than 200 anti-globalization groups is dedicated to reforming the policies and practices of the two international financial institutions. On its Web site the network provides fact sheets and international debt-relief articles, including fact sheets *Africa Needs Debt Cancellation, Not More IMF Programs* and *IMF/WB Debt Plan: Still Failing After All These Years.*

### Global Exchange

2017 Mission St., Suite 303, San Francisco, CA   94110
(415) 255-7296 • fax: (415) 255-7498
Web site: www.globalexchange.org

Founded in 1988, this nonprofit research, education, and action center seeks to link people in the North (First World) and South (Third World) who are promoting social justice and democratic development. Global Exchange promotes a U.S. foreign policy that is noninterventionist. It publishes *Global Exchanges* quarterly.

## Global Policy Forum (GPF)

777 UN Plaza, Suite 7G, New York, NY    10017
(212) 557-3161 • fax: (212) 557-3165
e-mail: globalpolicy@globalpolicy.org
Web site: www.globalpolicy.org

Global Policy Forum monitors policymaking at the United Nations, promotes accountability of global decisions, educates and mobilizes citizen participation, and advocates on vital issues of international peace and justice. The forum publishes policy papers and the *GPF Newsletter*. On its Web site, GPF provides an internal globalization link with subcategories on the topic, including politics, culture, and economics. The Web site provides charts, graphs, and articles, including *Measuring Globalization: Who's Up, Who's Down?*

## Global Trade Watch (GTW)

215 Pennsylvania Ave. SE, Washington, DC    20003
(202) 546-4996
Web site: www.tradewatch.org

GTW promotes democracy by challenging corporate globalization, arguing that the current globalization model is neither a random inevitability nor "free trade." GTW works on an array of globalization issues, including health and safety, environmental protection, economic justice, democratic, and accountable governance. GTW publishes the book *Whose Trade Organization? A Comprehensive Guide To the WTO*. Fact sheets and articles such as *Our World Is Not for Sale*, are available on its Web site.

## Greenpeace
Ottho Heldringstraat 5, Amsterdam    1066 AZ
  The Netherlands
Tel: +31 20 7182000 • fax: +31 20 5148151
e-mail: supporter.services@int.greenpeace.org
Web site: www.greenpeace.org/

Greenpeace is a global nonprofit organization and advocacy group that focuses on the most crucial worldwide threats to the planet's biodiversity and environment. Its Web site lists numerous environmental position papers and other publications relating to globalization and the environment. Recent publications include *Deadly Subsidies, The US Assault on Biodiversity—The WTO Dispute on GMOs,* and *Trading Away Our Last Ancient Forests.*

## The Heritage Foundation
214 Massachusetts Ave. NE, Washington, DC    20002
(202) 546-4400 • fax: (202) 546-0904
e-mail: info@heritage.org
Web site: www.heritage.org

The Heritage Foundation is a conservative think tank that supports the principles of free enterprise and limited government. Its many publications include the quarterly magazine *Policy Review* and the occasional papers series *Heritage Talking Points.* On its Web site, the foundation includes articles on globalization such as *Why America Needs to Support Free Trade* and *Emerging Global Menace?*

## Institute for International Economics (IIE)
1750 Massachusetts Ave. NW, Washington, DC    20036
(202) 328-9000 • fax: 202-659-3225
Web site: www.iie.com

A pro-globalization research institution devoted to the study of global macroeconomic issues, investment, and trade, IIE has contributed to the development of the World Trade Organization and the North American Free Trade Agreement and other initiatives. The Institute publishes policy papers and books on globalization including *Trade Policy and Global Poverty.* Some speeches and articles are available on its Web site, including *Globalization and the International Financial System.*

## International Forum on Globalization
1009 General Kennedy Avenue #2, San Francisco, CA 94129
(415) 561-7650 • fax: (415) 561-7651
e-mail: ifg@ifg.org
Web site: www.ifg.org

The International Forum on Globalization is an alliance of sixty leading activists, scholars, economists, researchers and writers formed to stimulate new thinking, joint activity, and public education in response to economic globalization. It publishes various reports, audio-tapes, books, and other publications relating to the effects of globalization. Recent publications include *China Copes with Globalization: A Mixed Review* and *Paradigm Wars: Indigenous Peoples' Resistance to Economic Globalization.*

## International Monetary Fund (IMF)
700 19th St. NW, Washington, DC 20431
Telephone Operator: (202) 623-7000 • fax: (202) 623-4661
e-mail: publicaffairs@imf.org
Web site: www.imf.org

The IMF is an international organization of 184 member countries. It was established to promote international monetary cooperation, exchange stability, and orderly exchange arrangements. IMF fosters economic growth and high levels of employment and provides temporary financial assistance to countries. It publishes the quarterly *Finance & Development* and reports on its activities, including the quarterly *Global Financial Stability Report*, recent issues of which are available on its Web site along with data on IMF finances and individual country reports.

## Peoples' Global Action (PGA)
c/o Canadian Union of Postal Workers (CUPW)
Ottawa, Ontario
  Canada
e-mail: agpweb@lists.riseup.net
Web site: www.agp.org

Peoples' Global Action is an alliance of grassroots organizations formed in 1998 to resist free trade and the World Trade Organization (WTO). The group has coordinated protests around the world to highlight the resistance to globalization. Its Web site contains information about various protest events as well as articles, bulletins, and links concerning various aspects of globalization in countries around the world.

## RAND Corporation
1776 Main Street, P.O. Box 2138
Santa Monica, CA   90407-2138
(310) 393-0411 • fax: (310) 393-4818
Web site: www.rand.org

RAND is a nonprofit think tank that conducts research and analysis on national security, business, education health, law, and science. Its Web site features a "Hot Topics" section on globalization that provides selected research, commentary, and congressional testimony by RAND experts on the topic.

## Ruckus Society
4131 Shafter Ave., Suite 9, Oakland, CA   94609
(510) 595-3442 • fax: (510) 763-7068
e-mail: info@ruckus.org
Web site: www.ruckus.org

The organization teaches nonviolent, civil disobedience skills to environmental and human rights organizations and helps other groups carry out "direct-action" protests. On its Web site, Ruckus publishes news articles on its activities from media supporters and opponents. The society publishes training manuals for nonviolent direct action, which are available on its Web site.

**Sierra Club**
85 Second Street, 2nd Floor, San Francisco, CA 94105
(415) 977-5500 • fax: (415) 977-5799
e-mail: information@sierraclub.org
Web site: www.sierraclub.org

The Sierra Club is a grassroots environmental organization with more than 750,000 members that works to protect the natural and human environments around the world. It publishes a bimonthly magazine, *Sierra*, and a newsletter, as well as numerous other publications. Its Web site contains reports and analyses of the effects of globalization, including *Taming Globalization for People and the Planet, Globalization is Heading the Wrong Way*, and *No Globalization Without Representation*.

**United Nations Development Programme (UNDP)**
One United Nations Plaza, New York, NY 10017
(212) 906-5315 • fax: (212) 906-5364
Web site: www.undp.org

UNDP funds six thousand projects in more than 150 developing countries and territories. It works with governments, UN agencies, and nongovernmental organizations to enhance self-reliance and promote sustainable human development. Its priorities include improving living standards, protecting the environment, and applying technology to meet human needs. UNDP's publications include the weekly newsletter *UNDP Flash*, the human development magazine *Choices*, and the annual *UNDP Human Development Report*. On its Web site, UNDP publishes the *Millennium Development Goals*, its annual report, regional data and analyses, speeches and statements, and recent issues of its publications.

**World Bank (IBRD)**
1818 H St. NW, Washington, DC 20433
(202) 477-1234 • fax: (202) 577-0565
Web site: www.worldbank.org

Formally known as the International Bank for Reconstruction and Development (IBRD), the World Bank seeks to reduce poverty and improve the standards of living of poor people around the world. It promotes sustainable growth and investments in developing countries through loans, technical assistance, and policy guidance. The World Bank publishes books on global issues, including *Global Economic Prospects 2005: Trade, Regionalism, and Development; Privatization in Latin America: Myths and Reality*; and *Intellectual Property and Development: Lessons from Recent Economic Research*. On its Web site, the World Bank provides current development data and programs.

**World Trade Organization (WTO)**
Centre William Rappard, Rue de Lausanne 154
Geneva 21   CH-1211
   Switzerland
(41-22) 739 51 11 • fax: (41-22) 731 42 06
e-mail: enquiries@wto.org
Web site: www.wto.org

WTO is a global international organization that establishes rules dealing with the trade between nations. Two WTO agreements have been negotiated and signed by the bulk of the world's trading nations and ratified in their parliaments. The goal of these agreements is to help producers of goods and services, exporters, and importers conduct their business. WTO publishes trade statistics, research and analysis, studies, reports, and the journal *World Trade Review*. Recent publications are available on the WTO Web site.

**Worldwatch Institute**
1776 Massachusetts Ave. NW, Washington, DC   20036-1904
(202) 452-1999 • fax: (202) 296-7365
e-mail: worldwatch@worldwatch.org
Web site: www.worldwatch.org

Worldwatch is a research organization that analyzes and calls attention to global problems, including environmental concerns such as the loss of cropland, forests, habitat, species, and water supplies. It compiles the annual State of the World anthology and publishes the bimonthly magazine *World Watch* and the World Watch Paper Series, which includes *Home Grown: The Case For Local Food In A Global Market* and *Underfed and Overfed: The Global Epidemic of Malnutrition.*

# Bibliography

J. Michael Adams and Angelo Carfagna
*Coming of Age in a Globalized World: The Next Generation.* Bloomfield, CT: Kumarian Press, 2006.

Janine Berg
*Miracle for Whom?: Chilean Workers Under Free Trade.* New York: Routledge, 2006.

Jeffry A. Frieden
*Global Capitalism: Its Fall and Rise in the Twentieth Century.* New York: W.W. Norton, 2006.

Thomas L. Friedman
*The Lexus and the Olive Tree.* New York: Anchor Books, 2000.

Thomas L. Friedman
*The World is Flat: A Brief History of the Twenty-first Century.* New York: Farrar, Straus and Giroux, 2005.

Anthony Giddens
*Runaway World: How Globalization Is Shaping Our Lives.* New York: Routledge, 2000.

Barry K. Gills and William R. Thompson
*Globalization and Global History.* New York: Routledge, 2006.

Patrick Hossay
*Unsustainable: A Primer for Global Environmental and Social Justice.* New York: Zed Books, 2006.

Will Hutton and Anthony Giddens, eds.
*Global Capitalism.* New York: The New Press, 2000.

Douglas A. Irwin
*Free Trade Under Fire.* Princeton, NJ: Princeton University Press, 2005.

| Robert A. Isa | *The Globalization Gap: How the Rich Get Richer and the Poor Get Left Further Behind.* Upper Saddle River, NJ: Prentice Hall/Financial Times, 2005. |

| John Micklethwait and Adrian Wooldridge | *A Future Perfect: The Essentials of Globalization.* New York: Crown Publishers, 2000. |

| James H. Mittelman | *The Globalization Syndrome: Transformation and Resistance.* Princeton, NJ: Princeton Univerity Press, 2000. |

| Heraldo Muñoz | *Democracy Rising: Assessing the Global Challenges.* Boulder, CO: Lynne Rienner Publishers, 2006. |

| Jamal R. Nassar | *Globalization and Terrorism: The Migration of Dreams and Nightmares.* Lanham, MD: Rowman & Littlefield, 2005. |

| Greg Palast | *The Best Democracy Money Can Buy.* Sterling, VA: Pluto Press, 2002. |

| George Soros | *George Soros on Globalization.* New York: Public Affairs, 2002. |

## Periodicals

| Hossein Askari | "Global Financial Governance: Whose Ownership?" *Business Economics*, April 2004. |

| Gary S. Becker | "When Globalization Suffers, the Poor Take the Heat," *Business Week*, April 21, 2003. |

| Aaron Bernstein | "Shaking Up Trade Theory," *Business Week*, December 6, 2004. |
| *Business Week Online* | "Globalization's Gloomy Guses Must Adapt," March 21, 2006. |
| Ian Campbell | "Retreat from Globalization," *The National Interest*, Spring 2004. |
| Michael Elliott | "A Backlash Against Globalization?" *Time International*, March 27, 2006. |
| Michael Elliott | "The Davos Man: Does Globalization Make the World Richer or Poorer?" *Time*, January 31, 2005. |
| Pete Engardio, Michael Arndt, and Dean Foust | "The Future of Outsourcing," *Business Week*, January 30, 2006. |
| *Foreign Policy* | "Measuring Globalization: Economic Reversals, Forward Momentum," March–April 2004. |
| *Geographical* | "Winners and Losers: Globalisation is a Complex Phenomenon with a Variety of Different Effects," October 2003. |
| Nigel C. Gibson | "Africa and Globalization: Marginalization and Resistance," *Journal of Asian and African Studies*, January–March 2004. |
| David Held | "Toward a New Consensus: Answering the Dangers of Globalization," *Harvard International Review*, Summer 2005. |

Douglas A.
Houston
"Can the Internet Promote Open Global Societies?," *Independent Review*, Winter 2003.

Paul Jeffrey
"Globalization is a 'Mutant Variety of Colonialism,' Activists Say," *National Catholic Reporter*, March 24, 2006.

Deborah
MacKenzie
"No Way to Run a World: Globalization is Happening Whether We Like It or Not," *New Scientist*, October 9, 2004.

Michael
Mosbacher and
Digby Anderson
"Dubious Moralisms," *New Criterion*, November 2002.

Joann Muller
"Surviving Globalism," *Forbes*, February 27, 2006.

Moises Naim
"The Five Wars of Globalization," *Foreign Policy*, January–February 2003.

Moises Naim
"Globalization: Passing Fad or Permanent Revolution?" *Harvard International Review*, Spring 2004.

Joaquina
Pires-O'Brien
"Globalization Now and Then," *Contemporary Review*, September 2002.

Jim Shultz
"People Power: Globalization Resistance Brings Down a President," *New Internationalist*, December 2003.

George Soros
"America's Global Role: Why the Fight for a Worldwide Open Society Begins at Home," *The American Prospect*, June 2003.

| Cynthia G. Wagner | "Coping with Globalization," *The Futurist*, January–February 2004. |
| Judy Wicks | "Our Mart, Not Wal-Mart: Is the Independently-owned Neighborhood Ice-cream Parlor the Real Alternative to Corporate Globalization?" *The Other Side*, January–February 2004. |

# Index

## A

Accountability, 120

Africa, 46–49, 61, 63–66

African National Congress (ANC), 48

Agricultural subsidies, 28–29, 48, 64–65

Agriculture
 globalization harms people involved in, 108–109
 mechanization of, 26

"Aid for trade," 64–65

AIDS epidemic, 46, 48

Air pollution, 89–90

Aldhous, Peter, 99–100

Amehou, Samuel, 66

Amnesty International, 158–159

Anderson, Kenneth, 161

Angola, 82

Antitrust agencies, 85–86

AOL, 150

Arif, Mohammed, 171

Auto industry, 36

## B

Baker, Dean, 58

Balko, Radley, 89

Bangladesh, 81, 165

Baran, Paul, 57

Bardham, Pranab, 78

Berman, Sheri, 173

Bhagwati, Jagdish, 70, 171

Bill & Melinda Gates Foundation, 86

Blood, David, 118

Botswana, 82

Brazil, 60–61, 76

Brecher, Jeremy, 92

Bretton Woods meeting (1944), 27, 103

Bureau of Labor Statistics, 31

Bush, George Sr., 132–133

Bush, George W., 153, 155, 172

Businesses. See Corporations; Multinational corporations

Buydens, Stephane, 184

## C

CAFE (Corporate Average Fuel Economy), 105–106

Capital flows, control over, 84–85, 182

Carbon dioxide emissions, 120

Cardoso, Fernando Henrique, 76

CEC. See North American Commission for Environmental Cooperation (NACEC)

CEDAW (Convention on the Elimination of All Forms of Discrimination Against Women), 159–160

Censorship, by Chinese government, 147–149

Central Intelligence Agency, 25

CERES (Coalition for Environmentally Responsible Economies), 120

Chemical industry, 97

Chicago Climate Exchange, 120

Child labor, 81

China
 benefits of globalization in, 20
 decline in poverty in, 80–81

213

democratization of, 174–175

opportunities for political dissent in, 146–149

outsourcing jobs to, 31

trade in goods by, 79

in the World Trade Organization, 172

China Internet Network Information Center (CNNIC), 147

Chinese Communist Party, 146

Chiquita banana case, 106

Chomsky, Noam, 170

Chua, Amy, 165

Clean Air Act, 105

Clinton, Bill, 133, 172

Coalition for Environmentally Responsible Economies (CERES), 120

Coffee market, 85

Commission on Environmental Cooperation, 144

Convention on the Elimination of All Forms of Discrimination Against Women (CEDAW), 159–160

Corporate Average Fuel Economy (CAFE), 105–106

Corporations

do not cause poverty and environmental degradation, 127–128

employment by foreign, 36

erosion of government to, 154–155

global governance and, 162–163

government's relationship with, 151–152

mergers of, 150–151

sustainable practices by, 119–121

unsustainable business practices by, 118–119

*see also* Multinational corporations

Costello, Tim, 92

**D**

DaimlerChrysler, 150

Dare, Sundoy, 47

DeLay, Tom, 172

Dell, 37

Democracy

ethnic violence caused by free market, 165–170

fading political systems and, 153–154

with free markets, 179–180

global governance *vs.*, 158

globalization directly promotes, 171

globalization is a danger to, 156

link between economic prosperity and, 172–173

opportunities for political dissent and, 146–149

role of middle class and, 173–174

threat of post-democracy to, 161–164

U.S. should promote, 180–181

wealth alone does not promote, 178–179

Developing countries

benefits of multinational investments in, 73–74

drive for cheap labor in, 25–26

environmental impact of free trade in, 93–95

environmental problems in, 122–123

ethnic realities of, 169, 170

failure of globalization in, 46–49

global trade talks discriminate against, 69

globalization causing economic disparities in, 51–53

globalization harms, 68–69

globalization has brought development to, 75–76

globalization reforms impacting, 58

impact of free trade on, 79–81

increasing economic sovereignty of, 56

international regulation for protecting, 53–54

lack of environmental standards in, 91–93

measures to help the poor in, 84–87

more globalization is needed for, 76–77

multinationals do not pay unfair wages in, 70–72

multinationals do not violate labor rights in, 72–73

open trade vs. environmental standards in, 129–130

opening markets by, 79

outsourcing jobs to, 31–32

participating in the Global New Deal, 57

pros and cons of globalization's effect on, 50

roots of poverty in, 81–83

slower economic growth for, 59–61

trade talks are unlikely to benefit, 66–67

transnational companies do not cause environmental harm in, 83–84

Diamond, Larry, 173

Doctors Without Borders, 86

Doha trade talks (2001), 63–64, 66–67

Dollar, David, 178

Dolphin-tuna dispute, 140–142

Downsizing, 30
See also Outsourcing

E

Eastern Europe, 89–90

Economic disparities
ethnic dimension of, 169–170
global, 110
increase in, 152–153

The Economic Freedom of the World (Gwartney/Lawson), 177

Economy, growth/development
benefits of globalization on, 20–21
in China, 146–147
decline in manufacturing jobs, 24–25
in developing countries, globalization has improved, 75–76
developing countries having slow, 59–61
energy use and, 96–97
environmental benefits of, 100
flexibility in, 38
global trade benefits U.S., 36–37
health and, 123–124
impact of globalization on, 19
link between democracy and, 172–173
trade restrictions stifle, 124–125
valued above environmental laws, 104–106
See also Global economy

Education, in developing countries, 61–62

Employment. See Jobs; Wages

Endangered Species Act (DATE), 105

English language, 21, 22

Enhanced Analytic Initiative, 120

Environment, globalization's effect on

along the Mexican-U.S. border, 131–132

corporations do not cause, 127–128

effect of trade liberalization on, 142–143

effects of export-oriented production on, 106–108

free trade protects, 122–130

future of economic development and, 98–101

globalization does not increase protection of, 102–103

human responsibility for management of, 101

impact of the twentieth century on, 97–98

is intrinsic to globalization, 102–103

long-run improvements in, 93–94

myths about trade and, 125–129

from NAFTA, 112–117

open *vs.* closed societies and, 89–91

opponents of globalization on, 22–23

in poor countries, 122–123

at regional and local levels, 108–109

sustainable business practices and, 119–121

trade agreements reinforced by protection of, 143–144

transnational companies do not harm, 83

unsustainable business practices cause, 118–119

Environmental damage/problems "Environmental Kuznets curve" (EKC) hypothesis, 112–113

Environmental standards

challenges against, 105–106

economic growth valued over, 104–105

lack of, 91–93

in Mexico, 115–116

NAFTA and, 144

open trade *vs.*, 129–130

should not take precedence over trade rules, 128–129

trade liberalization and, 141–142

Equator Principles, 120–121

Eskeland, Gunnar, 83

Ethnic violence, 165, 166–167

Europe, agricultural subsidies by, 28–29, 48

**F**

Fonte, John, 156

Ford Motor Company, 111, 150

Frank, Thomas, 169

Free market/trade

capital control flows and, 182

in China, 146–147

debate on impact of, 79–80

decline in poverty from, 80–81

democracy accompanies, 179–180

economists favoring, 33–34

enlarges markets for U.S. goods, 36–37

environmental effects of export-oriented production from, 106–108

environmental harm from, 93

environmental standards and, 90–92

fosters political freedoms, 176–179

"green ceiling" theory and, 93–94

hurts the poor, 68–69

myths about the environment and, 125–129

protects the environment, 122–130

U.S. should promote, 180–181

will lead to better environmental protection, 129–130

See also North American Free Trade Agreement (NAFTA)

Free Trade Area of the Americas Agreement (FTAA)

addressing environmental concerns over, 139–140

creation of, 104

environmental legislation accompanying, 144

Free Trade Under Fire (Irwin), 89

Freedom House, 180

Friedman, Thomas, 165

Fukuyama, Francis, 21

**G**

G-7 (Group of 7), 58

Gallagher, Kevin P., 67, 68, 112

Garment industry, 81

Garnett, Mark, 18

Gates, Bill, 153

GDP (Gross Domestic Product) growth

measuring environmental damage and, 113

slowdown of, in developing countries, 60–61

General Agreement on Tariffs and Trade (GATT), 103–104, 139, 140–141

General Electric, 119–120

General Motors (GM), 111, 150

Generalized System of Preferences (GSPs), 55

Gerstacker, Carl, 162

Glaxo Wellcome, 150

Glaxo-SmithKline, 150

Glewwe, Paul, 71–72

Global economy

agricultural subsidies and, 28–29

communication advancements and, 26–27

environmental impact of growth in, 98–101

failure of global institutions and, 27–28

global New Deal for, 54–57

green revolution and, 26

growth of, 96–97

prospects for improvement in, 29

transport activity in, 107–108

Global Freedom to Trade Campaign, 122

Global institutions. See International institutions

Global New Deal, 54–57

Global trade. See Free market/trade

Global Village or Global Pillage (Brecher/Costello), 92

Global warming, 56

Globalization

benefits of, 20–21

causes of, 18–19

complexity of, 23

debate over, 18, 41, 50, 78

is a human creation, 103

misguided criticism of, 169–170

people benefiting from, 109–111

perils of, 21–23

See also Free market/trade

*Globalization, Growth and Poverty: Building an Inclusive World Economy* (World Bank), 77

*Globalization, Poverty and Inequality* (Progressive Policy Institute), 76

Gore, Al, 118, 153

Government
censorship by Chinese, 147–149
constraints on, are desirable, 186–187
free market bring freedoms in, 176–177
global, 157–160
globalization does not decrease necessity of, 187–188
impact of globalization on, 19, 188–189
income redistribution by, 185
inflationary monetary policy by, 185–186
relationship with businesses, 151–152
as subordinate to business, 154–155
taxation by, 183–185
weakening of, 182
*See also* Democracy; Policy

Great Depression, the, 54

"Green ceiling" theory, 93–94

Green Revolution, 26, 86

Greenhouse gas emissions, 56

Griswold, Daniel T., 93, 176

Grossman, Gene, 93–94

Gwartney, James, 177

**H**

Harrison, Ann, 83

Hart, Stuart, 119

Health, in developing countries, 61

Hertz, Noreen, 150

HIV/AIDS, 48

Honda, 36

Hong Kong Doha talks (2005), 64–65

Hoover, Herbert, 54

Hu Jintao, 146, 148

Human rights issues, 158–159

Human Rights Watch, 158–159

**I**

IBM, 30–32

IKEA, 72

Imade, Lucky O., 50

Immigration reform, 86–87

Immigration, Western attitude toward, 22

Income. *See* Wages

India
decline in poverty in, 80
outsourcing jobs to, 30, 31
as role model for Middle East, 165
trade in goods by, 79

Indonesia, 80, 174

INEGI (National Institute for Statistics, Geography, and Information Systems, 113–114, 116

Infant mortality rates, 77

Inflationary monetary policy, 184–185

Information technology
offshoring's effect on, 37
outsourcing jobs in, 30

Integrated program for commodities (IPC), 55

Interdependency, 20

International Bank for Reconstruction and Development, 27

International division of labor, 52, 53–54

International institutions
  changing decision-making process in, 55
  economic reforms by, 58
  failure of, 27–28
  relationship between nongovernmental organizations and, 160–161
International Monetary Fund (IMF), 27
  on benefits of globalization, 77
  changing decision-making process in, 55
  creation of, 103–104
  economic reforms by, 58
  policies on global trade by, 47
International regulation, 53–54
Internationalization of capital, 53
Internet
  tax collection and, 184–185
  used in China, 147–149
Internet Corporation for Assigned Names and Numbers (ICANN), 148
Iran, 75
Iraq war, 159
Irwin, Douglas, 89, 91
Ivory Coast, 83

**J**

Jamaica, 82
Japan, 91
Jiang Zemin, 146
Jobs
  creation of U.S., 35–36
  decline in U.S. manufacturing, 24–25
  emergence of new, 38
  exaggeration of losses in, 41–42
  globalization producing U.S., 35–36
  greater productivity's impact on, 37–38
  number of lost, to offshoring, 35
  public policy addressing displacement of, 42–44
  See also Wages; Workers
Joffe-Walt, Benjamin, 148
Johnson, Nathan, 139
La Jolla Agreement (1992), 141

**K**

Kabeer, Naila, 81
Keynes, John Maynard, 118
Kraay, Aart, 178
Kristof, Nicholas, 72–73, 148
Krueger, Alan, 93–94
Krugman, Paul, 141–142
Kwa, Aileen, 65

**L**

Latin America, 60–61
Lawson, Robert, 177
Less developed countries (LDCs). See Developing countries
Life expectancy, 61, 77
Linz, Juan, 174
Lipset, Seymour Martin, 172
Liz Clairborne, 71

**M**

Maastricht Agreement, 104
Mahmud, Simeen, 81
Mandela, Nelson, 47
Mander, Jerry, 102
Mannesmann, 150

Manufacturing
    decline in jobs with, 24–25
    reemployment of workers in,
        44
Manzella, John L., 75
Mao Zedong, 146
Marine Mammal Protection Act
    (1972), 105, 141
Mauritius, 82
Mbeki, Thabo, 47, 49
McCain-Feingold bill, 153
McKibben, Bill, 98
Mercedes-Benz, 36
Mexico
    economic integration with the
        U.S., 131
    need for strong environmental
        institutions in, 115–116
    transnational countries do not
        choose to invest in, 83
    tuna-dolphin dispute and, 141
    *See also* North American Free
        Trade Agreement (NAFTA)
Mitsubishi, 111
Morocco, 83
Morris, David, 107
Motorola, 162–163
Mugabe, Robert, 167–168
Multinational corporations
    benefits of investments by,
        73–74
    communication advancements
        and, 26–27
    creation of overseas jobs by,
        36
    do not cause harm to the en-
        vironment, 83–84
    do not pay unfair wages,
        70–72
    do not violate labor rights,
        72–73
    drive for cheap labor by, 25–
        26, 27
    economic disparities and,
        110–111
Murdoch, Rupert, 150, 155

**N**

Nader, Ralph, 162
NAFTA. *See* North American Free
    Trade Agreement (NAFTA)
Nation state. *See* Government
National Audobon Society, 137
National Bureau of Economic Re-
    search, 76
National Institute for Statistics,
    Geography, and Information Sys-
    tems (INEGI), 113–114, 116
Natural resources, 126–127
Nature Conservancy, 101
New Deal, 54–57
News Corporation, 151
News media, 20
Nike, 71
Nongovernmental organizations
    (NGOs), 157, 158–161
North American Agreement on
    Environmental Cooperation
    (NAAEC), 133–138
North American Commission for
    Environmental Cooperation
    (NACEC), 116, 134, 136–137
North American Free Trade Agree-
    ment (NAFTA)
    creation of, 104
    efforts to address environ-
        mental harm from, 133–138
    environmental community's
        opposition to, 132
    environmental degradation
        from, 112–115
    environmental lessons from,
        116–117

environmental side agreement in, 144

has increased environmental awareness, 144

improvement in Mexico's air quality after, 94

need for environmental protection with, 115–116

North Korea, 75

Novartis, 36

Novo Nordisk, 120

**O**

Ocean shipping, 108

OECD (Organization for Economic Cooperation), 41–42, 99, 183

Office work, 35–36

Official Development Assistance (ODA), 55

Offshoring

explained, 34–35

information technology effected by, 37

policies helping U.S. workers due to, 38–40

*One Market under God* (Frank), 169

Organization for Economic Cooperation (OECD), 41–42, 99, 183

Outsourcing

explained, 34

staggering proportions of, 30–31

U.S. job market impacted by, 32

*See also* Offshoring

**P**

Pakistan, 75

Palley, Thomas, 68–69

Parry, Robert T., 33

Pesticide use, 97

Pharmaceutical companies, 86

Philippines, 82, 92

Plattner, Marc, 156

Policy

addressing job displacement, 42–44

environmental, 143–144

helping U.S. workers, 38–40

inflationary, 184–185

NAAEC has helped influence, 136–138

raising living standards in developing countries, 62

Political scandals, 153

Poor countries. *See* Developing countries

Population growth, 96

Poverty

corporations do not cause, 127–128

decline in, 80–81

local roots of, 81–83

measures to reduce, 84–87

trade helps to eliminate, 123–124

*Principles of Political Economy and Taxation* (Ricardo), 26

Progressive Policy Institute, 76

Prystay, Chris, 171

**R**

"Race to the bottom," 27, 91–93, 125

Regional Greenhouse Gas Initiative, 120

Regulation, need for international, 53–54

*See also* Environmental standards

Research, reducing poverty with, 86

Ricardo, David, 26
Rodrik, Dani, 56
Roosevelt, Franklin D., 55
Rosnick, David, 58
Russia, 173

**S**

Sanctions, trade, 125–126
Schuknecht, Ludger, 183
Seattle (WA) protest (1999), 29
September 11th terrorist attacks, 54, 159, 165
Sierra Club, 92, 140
Silva Reservoir (Mexico), 137
Smith Kline Beecham, 150
Social programs, 86, 185
South Africa, 47–48
South Korea, 82, 174
Soviet Block countries, former, 89–90, 179–180
Soviet Union, former, 89–90
Speth, James Gustave, 96
Stepan, Alfred, 174
Stiglitz, Joseph, 69
Sub-Saharan Africa, 61
Subsidies, agricultural, 28–29, 48, 64–65
Swaim, Paul, 41

**T**

Taliban, 152
Tanzi, Vito, 183
Taxation
    constraints on government for, 183–185
    redistributive, 185
Technology
    farming impacted by improvements in, 26
    fewer employees and, 25

globalization caused by, 18–19
influencing impact of globalization, 52
    *See also* Information technology; Internet
Tiananmen Square demonstration (Beijing)(1989), 146
Time Warner, 150
Tinbergen, Jan, 143–144
Torres, Raymond, 41
Toyota, 36
Trade. *See* Free market/trade
Trade agreements, reinforced by environmental protections, 143–144
Trade liberalization
    environmental impact of, 142–143
    environmental standards and, 141–142
    *See also* Free market/trade
Trade talks
    Africa's concerns in, 64
    discriminate against developing countries, 69
    Doha, 63–64
    Hong Kong, 64–65
    unlikely to benefit poor countries, 66–67
Transparency International, 120
Trust-busting, 85–87
Tuna-dolphin dispute, 140–142
Tyler, Gus, 24

**U**

Underdeveloped countries. *See* Developing countries
Unemployment, 24, 31
United Nations (UN), 46
United Nations Conference on Trade and Development (UNCTAD), 68

agricultural subsidies by, 48

changing decision-making process in, 55

Development program 1999 report, 110

post-democratic government and, 161

United Nations International Conference on Financing for Development (2002), 25

United States

agricultural subsidies by, 28–29

concentration of wealth in, 110–111

economic integration with Mexico, 131

global trade enlarges markets for goods in, 36–37

globalization produces jobs in, 35–36

impact of outsourcing on, 32

insourcing of jobs in, 35–36

in a post-democratic society, 163–164

tuna-dolphin dispute and, 141

U.S. Commerce Department, 36

U.S. Energy Information Agency, 99

Uruguay Round, 63–64, 69

V

Vega-Canovas, Gustavo, 131

Venezuela, 83

Vietnam, 71–72

Vodafone, 150

W

Wages

disparities in, 152–153

of displaced U.S. manufacturing workers, 44

free trade creates higher, 81

globalization creates cheap, 25

minimum, vs. manufacturing, 24

multinational corporations do not pay unfair, 70–72

trade leads to higher, 125

Wall Street, 31–32

Wallach, Lori, 170

Wal-Mart, 150

Water pollution, 94

Water supply, 99–100

Weapons trade, 22

Weisbrot, Mark, 58

Welfare spending, 185

White-collar jobs, 31–32

Whole Foods, 120

Wise, Timothy, 67

Wolf, Martin, 182

Workers

multinational do not violate labor rights of, 72–73

policies helping U.S., 38–40

reemployment of manufacturing, 44

See also Wages

World Bank

changing decision-making process in, 55

creation of, 27, 103–104

on developing countries, 77

on Doha trade talks, 66, 67

economic reforms by, 58

on environmental damage, 94

on Mexican environmental law, 115

on multinationals, 74

on pollution, 91

World Economic Forum, 90

World Resources Institute, 120

World Trade Organization (WTO)

changing decision-making process in, 55

China's entry in, 172

creation of, 104

Doha Development Agenda, 55

Doha trade talks and, 63, 74

environmental laws challenged by, 105, 106

on need for increased globalization, 75–76

protest against, 29

regulations of, 139

World Water Development Report (United Nations), 99

WuDunn, Sheryl, 72–73

**Z**

Zedillo, Ernesto, 76

Zimbabwe, 167–168